3/6

EURIPIDES

Hecuba

*Partly in the Original and partly
in Translation*

WITH INTRODUCTION AND NOTES BY

J. T. SHEPPARD, M.A., Litt.D.

FELLOW OF KING'S COLLEGE, CAMBRIDGE

OXFORD
AT THE CLARENDON PRESS
1924

Oxford University Press

London   *Edinburgh*   *Glasgow*   *Copenhagen*
New York   *Toronto*   *Melbourne*   *Cape Town*
Bombay   *Calcutta*   *Madras*   *Shanghai*
Humphrey Milford Publisher to the UNIVERSITY

Printed in England

EDITOR'S NOTE

THE study of Greek Tragedy may serve not merely to encourage accuracy but at once to feed and to discipline the imagination. I have therefore given the reader such help as I can not only for accurate construing but for appreciation of the play as a work of art. How far I have succeeded, the reader will decide. I have at any rate convinced myself that the *Hecuba* deserved the popularity which it enjoyed at the Renaissance, that it is a well-constructed play, and that the mobled Queen is not, as many critics have suggested, an irrelevant and eccentric moralizer.

I desire to thank the learned Reader of the Clarendon Press for saving me from several blunders. Except in a few passages I have followed Professor Murray's text.

INTRODUCTION

I. The Poet and the Theatre

Aristophanes makes great play with a mysterious joke about the mother of Euripides. He says she was a greengrocer. No one knows why, and it really does not matter. What does matter is, that Euripides was a free-born Athenian citizen, acquainted with all the great Athenians of his time, and that he had means and leisure to spend a great part of his life in writing plays. He was himself a student of men and books, rather than a man of action, though no Athenian citizen was allowed to shirk his part in the management of the Empire. Euripides was no exception to the rule by which citizens were liable for military service in the best forty years of their lives. Born in the year of Salamis 480 B.C. (though another account dates his birth four years earlier), he lived through the great days of Pericles, on into the terrible years of the war with Sparta and her allies, and died in exile just before the final Athenian disasters. His life cannot have lacked adventure.

But he hated war and politics, though he knew the ways of both. Fortunately Athens cared for art and poetry as well. Every year, at the festivals of Dionysus, but especially at the Great Dionysia in March, there were competitions between poets, lyric and dramatic. Rich citizens, as an honourable duty, paid the expenses.

A high magistrate, the Archon, chose three tragic poets to compete, and each of these produced four plays—three tragedies and one satyric drama (e. g. the *Cyclops*). Thus it was an honour even to compete. A board of (probably five) judges decided on the merits of the performances, and each competitor received a prize. The poet was responsible not only for the words, but for the music and the training of actors and singers, so that the whole performance had a unity of effect often lacking in our own theatre, where an author often sees his work produced with irrelevant music and by actors who are not in touch with his ideas.

The audience sat in the open air, on benches rising in tiers up the lower slopes of the Acropolis. Below them was the 'orchestra', or dancing-floor, on which the chorus performed. Beyond the 'orchestra' stood the 'skene', a wooden building, at first used simply as a changing-room for actors, but, at the time when Euripides produced his plays, already forming part of the imaginary scene, and painted to represent a palace or temple or some other imposing building. For the rustic 'satyric' drama, and occasionally for tragedy, it was modified to represent the mouth of a cave, or to suggest a country scene. But generally in tragedy the background was a palace-like structure, formal, no doubt, and beautiful, but quite familiar to the audience, and used again and again for many plays. The drama itself explains what, on each occasion, the 'skene' is supposed to represent.

This simplicity of setting was not altogether a disadvantage for the author. His audience would not be distracted by the scenery from the play. Their imagination would be alert, to supply whatever the poetry suggested. And there is one detail in the fixed scene which is of great dramatic value, namely the central door— a great double door which opens and shuts as the characters pass out and in. In our present play, the old Queen entices her victim through this central door into the hut where he is to be blinded, and his children murdered. The doors shut behind him, and before we hear his cry, we know he is doomed. One of the many sources which gave hints to early tragic composers was the ritual of lamentation at the tombs of great departed heroes. The palace door in these plays is often a gateway to death.

The actors wore masks, conventional and impressive. The origin of the custom was probably religious, but the effect in a play like the *Hecuba* must have been artistic. Hecuba, acted by a modern actress in a realistic make-up, would appear grotesque, if not actually disgusting, in her transformation from a proud, unfortunate Queen, to a grimacing, hideous Fury. Certainly, in a realistic modern make-up, Polymestor when he rushes out blinded, would be in danger of making horror eclipse the beauty of the poetry. The mask, conventionalizing the appearance of the actors, prevents grimacing, allows imagination free play, and sustains the tragic, but beautiful effect of the words.

Finally, the spectacle was certainly made magnificent by the use of splendid costume. In the present play, we see, first Hecuba and the Trojan captives, then Odysseus and his guards; later on come Polymestor and a barbaric array of Thracian soldiers; finally, Agamemnon and a Greek bodyguard fill up the picture. There is no lack of pageantry. Yet the main action is concentrated on one figure, Hecuba, now alone, now pleading with Odysseus while Polyxena listens, now uncovering the body of her son, now humiliating herself to Agamemnon, now confronting her treacherous enemy. The interest of the spectators is never divided from the main story: the setting, simple but magnificent, is a setting, not a distraction.

II. The Story of the Play

Such was the theatre for which Euripides composed his plays.[1] We have now to consider for a moment the theme he has chosen for his *Hecuba*, and to ask what sort of play he has made out of that theme.

For Athenians of the fifth century the Siege of Troy was the first great exploit of Greek history. Every Athenian boy knew Homer well, and some of them even knew the *Iliad* and *Odyssey* by heart. The tales of Homer's heroes were the inspiration both of poetry and of patriotism, proudly remembered by the men of Salamis and Athens when they rowed their galleys up the Hellespont, past Troy, past Sestos and Abydos in the narrows, on to Byzantium and Chalcedon, the great corn-cities at the gates of the Black Sea. On their right, as they entered the Straits, on Cape Sigeion, was the tomb of great Achilles ; and presently, on the right again, the mouth of Scamander, the plain and hill of Troy, and the tomb of their own hero, Ajax. Presently, on the left, on the shore of the promontory which we call Gallipoli (their 'Thracian Chersonese '), they saw a monument known as Hecuba's grave, and strangely called 'the Dog's Tomb' (Kynossema). In ancient days, as now, the rapid current of the Dardanelles, meeting the south-west winds at the mouth of the Straits, made voyaging no easy matter, and Athenian ships on the homeward voyage must often have stayed weatherbound upon this coast. At such a time we can imagine them discussing the old tale of the departure of the Achaean chiefs from Troy, of the adverse winds that would not let them sail, and of the dreadful sacrifice they offered at

[1] For a more detailed account, see the section contributed by Mr Cyril Bailey, p. 15.

Achilles' tomb.   Some would say that Hecuba, the Queen of Troy, went mad with grief when her child Polyxena was sacrificed.   But others had another story; it was not grief for Polyxena, the victim, after all, of superstition, not of merely wanton cruelty.   What changed the Queen into a mad avenging spirit was the treachery of a friend, more cruel than all the wrongs inflicted by her enemies, the Greeks.   Polymestor, King of the Thracians, in the old days when the Chersonese belonged to the barbarians, was the friend of Troy; and to him Priam had entrusted Polydorus, his youngest son, believing in his friendship. When Troy fell the Thracian killed the boy.   Hecuba learnt the truth, avenged her child, and was transformed into a fiend of vengeance.   That is why her monument is on the Thracian side of the Hellespont : and some will have it that her spirit, in the shape of a mad dog with flaming eyes, is still seen haunting the beaches and the gullies of the Chersonese.

III.   The Poet's Treatment of the Story

That, or something like it, is the story which Euripides took as his theme.   How has he treated it ?

He has transmuted the strange legend into a drama so realistic that, while we watch the play, we can accept, without question, whether we believe in miracles or not, the transformation of the Queen, which is prophesied at the end.   His Hecuba, for all her pride of royal birth and noble intellect, is transformed (not simply by the cruelty of her enemies and of circumstance, but by her own passion) into a veritable fiend.

At the beginning, though she is a slave, humiliated, physically broken, helpless; though Hector and her many valiant sons have fallen in battle; though her husband Priam has been murdered, her home destroyed, and her city sacked before her eyes, she is still strong in spirit. Her love for her surviving children, Polydorus and, above all, Polyxena, still keeps her human. Her love is also very proud. In her own eyes, and in the eyes of her Polyxena, she is still a Queen. She has her honour still.

She is a Queen, and hates democracy. She scorns the rhetoric and the sophistry of democratic leaders like Odysseus. She has pride of intellect also, and despises, as she fears, the passions by which the crowd are swayed. In her tragedy she has to gain her ends by using the very sophistries that she despises. Swept by a savage lust for vengeance, she becomes more cruel than any mob. In the end she loses her moral, though not her intellectual faculties under the strain. She becomes, essentially, almost, not quite, a wild beast. As we watch her in the terrible conflict with Polymestor, as we see her gloating over her successful vengeance, and listen to the cynical, inhuman cleverness of her final argument with Agamemnon, we realize that she has lost her soul. We are reminded of the curse in Meredith's fantastic *Woods of Westermaine*, the magic forest of life. Fair is the forest, if the wanderer be true to his best self : but if we take life wrongly, then the curse may be let loose :

> Beauty of her tresses torn,
> Shrieks as nature's maniac ;
> Hideousness on hoof and horn
> Tumbles, yapping on her track ;
> Haggard Wisdom, stately once,
> Leers fantastical . . .

Such is Hecuba's condition in the last part of the tragedy. In the first part, the unselfishness, the heroic beauty of Polyxena prevail over all wrongs. Polyxena, like her mother, is proud : but unlike Hecuba she is free from hatred, and she keeps her honour. Her suffering (how-ever indefensible the cause) is not intolerable, nor fatal to her spirit. By her noble bearing she saves, for the moment, Hecuba as well. Indefensible her sacrifice is : and so the Athenian audience would think. Like the other Trojan women, she had been taken by the Greeks from sanctuary, and her life should have been sacred. The Greeks attempt to justify their crime as an acknowledgement of the undoubted debt of gratitude they owe Achilles. But in fact they stand condemned by their own law, as Hecuba reminds Odysseus. There is, indeed, an analogy between this sacrifice to superstition and Hecuba's wild vengeance. 'We must honour our dead', cry the Greeks : and they kill Polyxena. 'I must avenge my dead', cries Hecuba : and she kills the innocent children of her enemy. No law, human or divine, can justify it. But Polyxena turns her tragedy into something noble, and saves Hecuba's humanity. In the sequel, the treacherous murder of Polydorus is fatal in effect. When Hecuba first realizes what has happened, she feels a change in her spirit, a devil of vengeance entering into her. At first she struggles against it. With her appeal for justice to Agamemnon, she reaches the highest moment of her spiritual struggle. Its refusal marks the crisis of her moral catastrophe. From that moment all her energies, all her great powers of mind, are concentrated in the plot for vengeance. The plot succeeds, but Hecuba has lost humanity. She has in fact, for the sake of vengeance, shut herself off from the eternal universal law in whose name she appealed to Agamemnon ; the law of which Cicero says 'he who will not obey it makes himself an exile from himself, and because he despises the nature of man must suffer by that very act the greatest of all penalties'. *Naturam hominis aspernata Hecuba hoc ipso luet maximas poenas.* When the Thracian prophesies that Hecuba is to become a mad dog, he adds nothing to her tragedy; for, in spirit, she has already suffered 'that bestial transformation'.

And yet the last note of the play is human. Hecuba had another son, whose fate is worse than that of Polydorus, and a daughter whose fate is worse than that of Polyxena. Polydorus is the victim of a treacherous ally: Helenus, the prophet, is a traitor to his country. Polyxena is sacrificed to Achilles; Cassandra is the slave of Agamemnon and is to be murdered with her master, by Clytaemnestra, his wife. At the end, though she can laugh at the Thracian's prophecy of her own transformation, Hecuba is still vulnerable, still human enough, to suffer when she learns Cassandra's destiny. That is the consummation of her tragedy, and after that revelation she is silent. In the early part of the play we care for Hecuba because Polyxena cares, and we love Polyxena. When we see her moving towards her vengeance, and away from human sympathy, we still care for Hecuba, because we care so much for Polyxena. And in the end, in spite of her appalling cruelty and cynicism, we understand and pity her because it is Cassandra's fate, and not her own, that breaks her heart.

Thus the play ends in pity, not in terror only. It is no mere collection of sensational episodes, no string of disconnected incidents, but a work of art, a poem of balanced composition, a story terrible indeed, but also beautiful. And the vision of life which the poet tried to show to his own countrymen in their time of war and trouble is a vision that is true to-day.

> The winds are high, and Helle's tide
>   Rolls darkly, heaving to the main;
> And Night's descending shadows hide
>   That field with blood bedew'd in vain,
> The desert of old Priam's pride;

> The tombs, with relics of his reign,
> All—save immortal dreams . . .[1]

The Hellespont, or Dardanelles, says Mr. Masefield, is 'the most important channel of water in the world'. It is important as the entrance to the Black Sea, the link or barrier between Europe and Asia, Russia, and the southern seas. It is more important, if mind is more than matter, for the memories it holds of human heroism. When Homer sang of Troy, three thousand years ago, he made the heroism of the Trojans and the Greeks alike immortal, and no traveller to-day can pass into the Hellespont without thoughts of the brave men who fought and suffered in the plain of Homer's 'windy Ilion'. Here Xerxes, in his youthful pride and confidence, reviewed the swarming hosts of Asia, passing the straits, as he believed, for the humiliation of Athens and the conquest of Greece. He wept, according to the story, at the thought of their mortality. Here Alexander the Great, at the beginning of his campaigns, paid homage to the memory of Homer and the valour of Achilles. And here, in our own times, a noble and most tragic struggle has been waged, amid strange perplexities, with triumphant, smiling courage, by heroes not less noble than the finest of the poet's dream. 'They went like Kings in a pageant to the imminent death.'[2]

Among them were many who knew little either of Homer or Greek tragedy, but some who loved Greek poetry. One of them, who died before the landing on Gallipoli, wrote in his note-book scraps of poetry like this:

> They say Achilles in the darkness stirred,
> And Hector, his old enemy,
> Moved the great shades that were his limbs. They heard
> More than Olympian thunder on the sea.

---

[1] Byron, *Bride of Abydos.*   [2] Masefield, *Gallipoli.*

And this :

> And Priam and his fifty sons
> Wake all amazed, and hear the guns,
> And shake for Troy again.[1]

We shall better understand the *Hecuba* if we remember
the men of Gallipoli as we read. Like Polyxena in our
play, they 'died as they had lived, owning no master
on this earth'. They cheered each other, and 'all was
beautiful in that gladness of men about to die, but the most
moving thing was the greatness of their generous hearts'.

The immortal dreams of the poet live on. They tell us
that, although the fate of men is inscrutable, and destiny
seems cruel, the freedom of the spirit is not subject to
destiny. Folly and wickedness, cruelty and superstition
still add to the confusion and the misery of the world.
Agamemnon temporizes, Odysseus schemes, and Polymestor clutches for his gold to-day, as in the days of
Euripides. And there are men and women who, like
Hecuba, think vengeance a solution. But Polyxena,
although she also suffers, triumphs in the strength of love.
The meaning of this play, as of so many of the greatest
tragic poems, is not that life is chaos, but that human love
and wisdom are symbols of a higher law than men have yet
devised :

> These are the spells by which to reassume
> An empire o'er the disentangled doom.
> To suffer woes which Hope thinks infinite ;
> To forgive wrongs darker than death or night ;
> To defy Power which seems omnipotent ;
> To love and bear, to hope till Hope creates
> From its own wreck the thing it contemplates.[2]

---

[1] Rupert Brooke, *Memoir*, pp. cl and cli.
[2] Shelley, *Prometheus Unbound.*

IV. DRAMATIC PERFORMANCES AT ATHENS [1]

In order to have a clear idea of the appearance of the play to an Athenian audience, we must obtain some notion of the nature and conditions of dramatic performances at Athens.

The Athenian drama arose out of and was always closely connected with the worship of Dionysus : tragedy is said to have developed from the dithyrambic hymns sung by a chorus in his honour, comedy from the more light-hearted songs associated with the phallic procession (κῶμος). The stages of development are not easy to trace, but by the beginning of the fifth century B.C. tragedy was completely established, and comedy, which had combined with the songs of the Dionysiac revel burlesque scenes of the kind traditional in the Peloponnese, won its full recognition soon afterwards. There were two annual festivals of Dionysus in Athens at which the performance of drama took place, the Great or City Dionysia in the month of Elaphebolion (March) and the Lenaea (the rural Dionysia of Athens) in Gamelion (February). The Great Dionysia was held in the precinct of Dionysus Eleuthereus on the south side of the Acropolis : tragedy was here the main interest, but there were also performances both of dithyrambs and of comedy. The Lenaea was a more domestic festival, held originally in the Lenaeum (whose site is disputed), but later, after the establishment of a permanent theatre, also in the precinct of Dionysus Eleuthereus : at this festival comedy became the most important element, though tragedy was also produced.

The dramatic performances took the form of competitions between poets. The authors who wished to compete applied to the Archon, who gave them a licence by ' granting a chorus ', and assigned to each a Choragus, a wealthy man who bore the expenses of the production.

[1] Mr. Cyril Bailey has kindly contributed this section for use in the series.

It was usual in tragedy for three poets to compete at each performance, each customarily producing a group of four plays, three tragedies (which Aeschylus, as in the *Oresteia*, often connected in subject as a 'trilogy') and one satyric drama. In comedy, on the other hand, it was the custom for five [1] poets to compete, each producing one play. The poet acted as 'producer' and instructed the chorus and actors : hence he is often referred to as the 'teacher' (διδάσκαλος). After the completion of the performance the prizes were awarded by judges (κριταί) appointed for the purpose (five in number in the case of comedy and probably also for tragedy) : each of the competing poets was awarded a prize, but they were arranged in order of merit and records were kept on stone of the results.

In order to imagine what the performances were like, we must forget all modern associations with indoor theatres. The performance took place out of doors on a round level space known as the 'dancing-place' (ὀρχήστρα), in the centre of which stood the altar (θυμέλη). The spectators sat on benches (ἴκρια) round the ring, and, as it was necessary to raise the circles of benches one above the other, it seems likely that from the first a hill-side was chosen, where the natural formation of the ground could be used. This is the case in the theatre at Athens, and after an accident with the benches in 499 B.C. the ground was dug out and raised in tiers to form a secure foundation, and thus the first permanent theatre was established. We have, then, always to think of the spectators not looking up, as from the stalls in a modern theatre, to a square stage above them, but looking down on the round orchestra below them.

We cannot be certain of the stages by which the choric

---

[1] During the Peloponnesian War the number of comic poets competing was for a few years reduced to three : when Aristophanes produced *The Clouds* he had only two competitors.

song became the drama, but it seems probable that at first in tragedy the leader of the chorus (*coryphaeus*) held dialogue with the rest of the chorus, and in the 'comus' with the bystanders. Later an independent actor was introduced. In tragedy this innovation is traditionally assigned to the ancient dramatist Thespis: Aeschylus is said to have introduced a second actor, making real dramatic dialogue possible, and Sophocles a third: beyond this the number was not, in the classical period, increased. Now all the plays which have come down to us contain more than three characters: it would therefore become necessary for the actors to have some kind of 'green-room' to which they might retire to change their dresses. This was provided for by the erection of a booth (σκηνή) across the end of the orchestra opposite to the hill-side. This was, no doubt, at first a temporary structure, but when the theatre became permanent took the form of a simple wooden building with doors, through which the actors might issue. In the later stone theatres, remains of which are still extant in several places in Greece and elsewhere, there is in front of the σκηνή an elaborate stage rising some ten feet above the orchestra. Excavations have proved conclusively that this did not exist in the fifth century, and it is a much disputed question whether there was any raised stage at all for the actors. On the one hand there is no doubt that there was easy communication between actors and chorus, and it is clear that certain scenes, in comedy at any rate, must have taken place entirely in the orchestra: on the other hand passages where actors are told to 'come up' seem to imply a raised platform. On the whole the most probable conclusion is that in the earliest permanent theatre a low platform (λογεῖον) ran in front of the whole of the σκηνή, communicating by two or three steps, also running the whole length, with the orchestra. At the two ends of this platform and between it and the seats of the audience would be left gangways (πάροδοι), by which the chorus entered the orchestra and actors came on, who were not represented

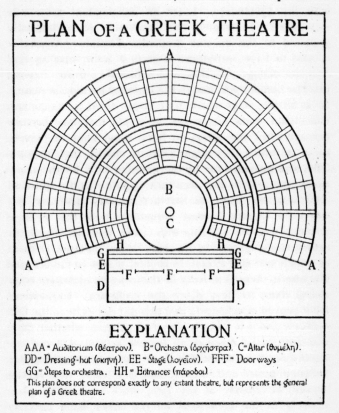

PLAN OF A GREEK THEATRE

EXPLANATION

AAA = Auditorium (θέατρον).   B = Orchestra (ὀρχήστρα).   C = Altar (θυμέλη).
DD = Dressing-hut (σκηνή).   EE = Stage (λογεῖον).   FFF = Doorways
GG = Steps to orchestra.   HH = Entrances (πάροδοι).
This plan does not correspond exactly to any extant theatre, but represents the general plan of a Greek theatre.

as issuing from a house. The general arrangements of the theatre might then be represented as on the plan.

At no period of the Attic drama was there any attempt at elaborate and realistic scenery, as on the modern stage. The audience did not require it and its effect would be quite lost at the distance at which many of them sat from the stage. In the earlier period the σκηνή was merely a retiring-room, and was not even thought of as a background; but about 460 B.C., it became customary to paint it so as to represent some sort of back-scene: for tragedy it would have columns and pillars so as to resemble a palace or temple, in comedy the decoration would be simpler and would represent one or more private houses.[1] For the satyric drama the scene would be some rustic place or wild spot, and we may suppose that a similar background would be used for tragedies whose scene was laid in the country. In the normal tragedy and comedy the exits from the σκηνή on to the stage would represent the doors of the palace, temple, or house. Some simple devices supplemented the scenery: (a) on certain occasions, particularly in comedy, the actors might appear on the roof of the σκηνή; (b) a machine, known as the *eccyclema*, was used to reveal action supposed to be taking place inside the palace or house: it was a platform, either turned round on a pivot or, more probably perhaps, rolled forward on wheels;[2] (c) a machine of some kind (μηχανή) was used to hoist up divine beings who were supposed to appear flying in the sky.[3] Scenery and devices all appear crude and inadequate to modern notions, but the Athenian audience, like the Elizabethan, had more imagination than ourselves and could supply what was wanting for themselves: in some modern revivals of Shakespeare's plays the simplification of scenery has been proved to heighten the dramatic effect.

On the other hand, if scenery was simple, dresses, in tragedy at any rate, were elaborate. The costume of

---

[1] In *The Clouds* the σκηνή must have been made to represent two houses, Strepsiades' home and the 'Thinking-School'.

[2] The *eccyclema* was probably used in *The Clouds* to reveal the interior of the 'Thinking-School' (184).

[3] This is parodied in *The Clouds* in the appearance of Socrates in his basket.

the tragic actor consisted of a long flowing robe of a conventional pattern with sleeves : the materials and ornaments used were of brilliant and gay colouring, which must have produced a striking effect of richness against the simple background and the stone floor of the orchestra. The tragic actor's figure was padded and he wore a long boot (κόθορνος) reaching almost to the knees. The comic actor wore exaggerated padding enclosed in a tight-fitting jersey, over which were the ordinary tunic and cloak of common life. The chorus were dressed, as a rule, in the ordinary Greek dress, varying according to the characters which they impersonated, but were sometimes attired in strange and outlandish garments, as, for instance, in the *Eumenides* of Aeschylus and the many comedies where the chorus represented animals or imaginary beings. But the strangest feature to our notions both in tragedy and comedy was that all the actors wore masks. This was almost certainly a ritual tradition, but it is said also to have assisted in making the actor's voice audible through the huge theatre. The masks would represent male and female characters, and no doubt, especially in comedy, there were traditional masks for different types of characters. The female parts as well as the male were invariably performed by men.

The chorus in tragedy usually consisted of fifteen, in comedy of twenty-four, and in each case had a leader (*coryphaeus*), who engaged in dialogue as their representative with the actors. They entered by the *parodos*, usually, it appears, by that on the right hand of the spectators. During the dialogue they faced the stage and so followed the words of the actors, but while they sang the choruses they moved about in dances, the evolutions of which are unknown to us. It may be noted, perhaps, that the attention of the audience would thus be transferred to the orchestra during the break in the action of the play, and away from the empty stage. In the earlier times of tragedy the chorus played an important part in the development of the story, but their importance gradually dwindled and Euripides sometimes uses the chorus as little more than 'incidental music' between the acts. The chorus of the Old Comedy, at any rate in Aristophanes' plays, retains its character as an actor in the drama, and not infrequently divides into two sections taking part with contesting actors on the stage.

This short sketch of the nature of the Athenian theatre is intended to suggest nothing more than the picture of the performance which readers of the Greek drama should have in mind. There are, of course, many further details which must be considered with reference to individual plays.

HECUBA

CHARACTERS OF THE PLAY
in the order of their appearance.

THE GHOST OF POLYDORUS.	ODYSSEUS.
HECUBA.	TALTHYBIUS.
CHORUS OF CAPTIVE TROJAN	HECUBA'S SERVING-WOMAN.
WOMEN.	AGAMEMNON.
POLYXENA.	POLYMESTOR.

The play was first produced in Athens, probably in the
year 425 B.C.

The scene is laid before the Head-quarters of AGAMEMNON *in
the Greek encampment on the Thracian Chersonese. Enter,
above, the* GHOST OF POLYDORUS.

ΠΟΛΥΔΩΡΟΥ ΕΙΔΩΛΟΝ

Ἥκω νεκρῶν κευθμῶνα καὶ σκότου πύλας
λιπών, ἵν' Ἅιδης χωρὶς ᾤκισται θεῶν,
Πολύδωρος, Ἑκάβης παῖς γεγὼς τῆς Κισσέως
Πριάμου τε πατρός, ὅς μ', ἐπεὶ Φρυγῶν πόλιν
κίνδυνος ἔσχε δορὶ πεσεῖν Ἑλληνικῷ,   5
δείσας ὑπεξέπεμψε Τρωικῆς χθονὸς
Πολυμήστορος πρὸς δῶμα Θρηκίου ξένου,
ὃς τήνδ' ἀρίστην Χερσονησίαν πλάκα
σπείρει, φίλιππον λαὸν εὐθύνων δορί.
πολὺν δὲ σὺν ἐμοὶ χρυσὸν ἐκπέμπει λάθρα   10
πατήρ, ἵν', εἴ ποτ' Ἰλίου τείχη πέσοι,
τοῖς ζῶσιν εἴη παισὶ μὴ σπάνις βίου.
νεώτατος δ' ἦ Πριαμιδῶν, ὃ καί με γῆς
ὑπεξέπεμψεν· οὔτε γὰρ φέρειν ὅπλα

οὔτ' ἔγχος οἷός τ' ἦ νέῳ βραχίονι.　15

ἕως μὲν οὖν γῆς ὄρθ' ἔκειθ' ὁρίσματα
πύργοι τ' ἄθραυστοι Τρωικῆς ἦσαν χθονὸς
Ἕκτωρ τ' ἀδελφὸς οὑμὸς εὐτύχει δορί,
καλῶς παρ' ἀνδρὶ Θρῃκὶ πατρῴῳ ξένῳ
τροφαῖσιν ὥς τις πτόρθος ηὐξόμην, τάλας·　20
ἐπεὶ δὲ Τροία θ' Ἕκτορός τ' ἀπόλλυται
ψυχή, πατρῷα θ' ἑστία κατεσκάφη,
αὐτὸς δὲ βωμῷ πρὸς θεοδμήτῳ πίτνει
σφαγεὶς Ἀχιλλέως παιδὸς ἐκ μιαιφόνου,
κτείνει με χρυσοῦ τὸν ταλαίπωρον χάριν　25
ξένος πατρῷος καὶ κτανὼν ἐς οἶδμ' ἁλὸς
μεθῆχ', ἵν' αὐτὸς χρυσὸν ἐν δόμοις ἔχῃ.
κεῖμαι δ' ἐπ' ἀκταῖς, ἄλλοτ' ἐν πόντου σάλῳ,
πολλοῖς διαύλοις κυμάτων φορούμενος,
ἄκλαυτος ἄταφος· νῦν δ' ὑπὲρ μητρὸς φίλης　30
Ἑκάβης ἀίσσω, σῶμ' ἐρημώσας ἐμόν,
τριταῖον ἤδη φέγγος αἰωρούμενος,
ὅσονπερ ἐν γῇ τῇδε Χερσονησίᾳ
μήτηρ ἐμὴ δύστηνος ἐκ Τροίας πάρα.

All the Greek army on this Thracian coast　35
Sits idle by the ships.　The son of Peleus,
Achilles, at the first plash of the oars
Dipped for the homeward voyage, out of the tomb
Appearing, bade them offer at his grave
Polyxena, my sister, for his glory.　40
And he shall have his will.　The boon he craves
Friendship will not refuse.　Polyxena,
So Destiny ordains it, dies to-day.

　The Mother shall behold, for her two children,
Two bodies dead, myself and that sad maid ;　45
For I too shall appear, flung by the waves
At a slave-woman's feet, and claim my burial.
This boon the princes of the dead concede me,
To find my mother's arms, and rest in the tomb :　50
That done, my prayers are granted, all my wish
Fulfill'd.　But see !　From Agamemnon's house

Comes the old Hecuba, by my apparition
Startled. I will not stay to trouble her.

[*The central door of the scene-building has opened, but at first
nothing can be seen in the darkness within.*]

Alas! Alas!
O Mother, Queen, from royal state how fallen   55
To days of bondage! All thy happiness
How changed to equal grief! Some jealous god
Deals thee for all thy joy full weight of present woe.

[*The* GHOST *vanishes. The voice of* HECUBA, *sometime
Queen of Troy, is heard within.*]

Hecuba. Bring me out of this place. Ah, children, I am
old.
Raise me, and bring me out. My Trojans, I was your
Queen,   60
    But now, with you, I am a slave.
Hold me; bear me up; come closer: clasp the old
hand, and lift me from the ground.
I too will do my share: I will lean on your arm: it
shall be as a staff for my feet: 65
So, slowly, step after step, I will struggle onward.

[HECUBA, *supported by Trojan women, has appeared in the
doorway. She now advances into the open sunlight.*]

O radiant Day, glory of the fire of Zeus! O darkness
of Night!
    Why am I troubled thus in the night
By terrors and phantoms haunted? O dread Earth,   70
    Mother of black-winged Dreams,
I cry it aloud to avert it, the vision reveal'd in a dream
of the night:
Dream that I dream't of my son, safe kept in Thrace,
Dream of my love, my daughter, Polyxena,   75
    Vision of terror.

ὦ χθόνιοι θεοί, σώσατε παῖδ' ἐμόν,
ὃς μόνος οἴκων ἄγκυρ' ἔτ' ἐμῶν   80
τὴν χιονώδη Θρῄκην κατέχει
ξείνου πατρίου φυλακαῖσιν.

ἔσται τι νέον·
ἥξει τι μέλος γοερὸν γοεραῖς.
οὔποτ' ἐμὰ φρὴν ὦδ' ἀλίαστος　　　　　85
φρίσσει, ταρβεῖ.
ποῦ ποτε θείαν Ἑλένου ψυχὰν
καὶ Κασάνδραν ἐσίδω, Τρῷάδες,
　　ὥς μοι κρίνωσιν ὀνείρους ;

This have I seen.　A wolf with bloody claw　　90
Tearing the throat of a dappled hind, torn from my
　　arms without pity.
　　　　　And this is my fear,
Haunting me still, since the ghost of Achilles came
　　Over the edge of the tomb,
And a Trojan woman, a daughter of sorrow, he sought
　　for his glory's prize.　　　　　95
　　Hear me, ye Spirits!　Give ear to my cry and
　　avert it!
　　Let not this fall on my child!

[*Rapt in her prayer,* HECUBA *has not noticed the approach of
the Chorus, a band of captive Trojan women, who have
come with news from another part of the camp.* HECUBA
*is the central figure in the picture, rigid, listening in
silence.*]

Chorus.

Hecuba, I am here!
From the tents of my bondage I come,
　　For a slave am I,
From the place by the lot and the will of a master ap-
　　pointed,　　　　　100
　　When they drove me from Troy,
As a beast that is caught by the hunter, the prize of the
　　Greeks, the prey of the spear.
　　No comfort I bring thee.
Only a burden of news, a message of sorrow.　　　105
　　Herald of grief am I.

ἐν γὰρ Ἀχαιῶν πλήρει ξυνόδῳ
λέγεται δόξαι σὴν παῖδ' Ἀχιλεῖ
σφάγιον θέσθαι· τύμβου δ' ἐπιβὰς

οἶσθ᾽ ὅτε χρυσέοις ἐφάνη σὺν ὅπλοις,   110
τὰς ποντοπόρους δ᾽ ἔσχε σχεδίας
λαίφη προτόνοις ἐπερειδομένας,
τάδε θωΰσσων·
Ποῖ δή, Δαναοί, τὸν ἐμὸν τύμβον
    στέλλεσθ᾽ ἀγέραστον ἀφέντες;   115

Then rose and clashed
Waves of strong dissension,
Opinion in the host of warrior Greeks blowing two
    ways,
For some would give the grave its victim, some re-
    fuse it.
    And in thy cause   120
    Zealous was Agamemnon
For the wild maid's sake, the prophetess, his bride.
    The sons of Theseus,
    Branches of Athens,
    Orators twain,
    But in judgement not divided,   125
Bidding them pour at the tomb of their Achilles
    The gift of the pure young blood,
Cried that the valour of great Achilles must be hon-
    oured
    More than Cassandra's bed.
So argument met argument, the scales still equal, till the
    host was won   130
By the words of the glib, the honeyed, the subtle contriver,
    the people's courtier, Odysseus:
    'Slight not the noblest of Greeks   135
    For a slave-girl's life:
In the realms of Persephone, let not the dead rise up and
    say "These Greeks
Have left the plains of Troy, and they knew no gratitude
    To Greeks who died for Greece".'   140
Very soon Odysseus will be here.
As a foal from the mother's breast he will snatch the
    child:
From the old arms he will take her, and lead her
    away.
    Get you to the shrines, to the altars!

Nay, sit at Agamemnon's feet, and cry aloud   145
    To the gods in Heaven, to the gods below the Earth.
      So, if thy prayer avail,
Thou shalt not mourn thy child of sorrow.
Or else, it is Destiny. Over the tomb thou needs must see
    her fall,   150
When the throat, once gay with gold, shall be stained with
    crimson,
    And the blood in a dark stream flow.

HECUBA (*who has remained motionless in the centre of
the picture*).

Ah me!   What sound of woe have I to utter?
    What use in clamour and lamenting?   155
Wretched am I for this weight of wretched age upon me,
    And my slavery, unbearable, intolerable.   Woe is
    me!
Is there any to help me?   What of my kinsmen now?
    What city have I?
    The old man gone, and gone my sons.   160
Which way shall I turn?   Whither betake me?
    Whither?
Is there any god or spirit to succour me?

ὦ κάκ' ἐνεγκοῦσαι,   165
Τρῳάδες ὦ κάκ' ἐνεγκοῦσαι
πήματ', ἀπωλέσατ' ὠλέσατ'· οὐκέτι μοι βίος
    ἀγαστὸς ἐν φάει.
ὦ τλάμων ἄγησαί μοι πούς,
    ἄγησαι τᾷ γηραιᾷ   170
πρὸς τάνδ' αὐλάν· ὦ τέκνον, ὦ παῖ,
δυστανοτάτας ματέρος—ἔξελθ' ἔξελθ'
οἴκων—ἄιε ματέρος αὐδάν.
ὦ τέκνον ὡς εἰδῇς οἵαν οἵαν   175
ἀίω φάμαν περὶ σᾶς ψυχᾶς.

[*Enter, from the house*, POLYXENA.]

Polyxena. Mother, what is it?   Mother, why do you call?
· What is the news that you cry so loud?
    Mother, I am afraid.

  Out of the house I come, like a startled bird.

Hecuba. Alas, ah me, my child?   180

Polyxena. What, nothing but sad words? Your news has
    an ill beginning.

Hecuba. Alas, it is . . . for your life . . .

Polyxena. Tell it me plainly. Do not hide it from me.
    I am afraid, afraid.
    Mother, why do you moan?   185

Hecuba. Child, alas, child of a mother of sorrow . . .

Polyxena. What mean you?

Hecuba. The victim—with one consent the Argives have
    decreed it—
    At the tomb to be offered to the son of Peleus. 190

Polyxena. Mother, what have you said?
    Ah me! What is this fate unenviable, evil?
    Tell me, tell me, mother.

Hecuba. Evil words, alas! Yet I will tell you.
    They bring me news that by a vote the Argives have
    determined . . .   195
    Alas for me! It is . . . your life.

Polyxena. Mother, whose life is only sorrow,
    Sufferer, who hast so much endured,
    How doth some terrible spirit heap on thee 200
    Anguish unspeakable.
    I shall no more be with thee, the sad child
    No more on thy sad age attendant
    Shall live, a slave with a slave.
    They will take me, thou shalt see it, 205
    As a heifer, fed on the hills,
    Sad mother, they will ravish me away.
    The knife will touch my throat, and I shall go into the
    darkness,
    And I shall lie in Hades with the dead. 210
    Mother, whose life is sorrow,
    My tears, my dirges are for thee.
    Since life for me brings only shame and anguish,
    I have no tears for life. It is a better fate for me to
    die.   215

   [*Enter from the camp* ODYSSEUS *attended.*]

Χο. καὶ μὴν Ὀδυσσεὺς ἔρχεται σπουδῇ ποδός,
  Ἑκάβη, νέον τι πρὸς σὲ σημανῶν ἔπος.

ΟΔΥΣΣΕΥΣ

γύναι, δοκῶ μέν σ᾽ εἰδέναι γνώμην στρατοῦ
ψῆφόν τε τὴν κρανθεῖσαν· ἀλλ᾽ ὅμως φράσω.
ἔδοξ᾽ Ἀχαιοῖς παῖδα σὴν Πολυξένην   220
σφάξαι πρὸς ὀρθὸν χῶμ᾽ Ἀχιλλείου τάφου.
ἡμᾶς δὲ πομποὺς καὶ κομιστῆρας κόρης
τάσσουσιν εἶναι· θύματος δ᾽ ἐπιστάτης
ἱερεύς τ᾽ ἐπέσται τοῦδε παῖς Ἀχιλλέως.
οἶσθ᾽ οὖν ὃ δρᾶσον ; μήτ᾽ ἀποσπασθῇς βίᾳ   225
μήτ᾽ ἐς χερῶν ἅμιλλαν ἐξέλθῃς ἐμοί·
γίγνωσκε δ᾽ ἀλκὴν καὶ παρουσίαν κακῶν
τῶν σῶν.   σοφόν τοι κἂν κακοῖς ἃ δεῖ φρονεῖν.

Εκ. αἰαῖ· παρέστηχ᾽, ὡς ἔοικ᾽, ἀγὼν μέγας,
πλήρης στεναγμῶν οὐδὲ δακρύων κενός.   230
κἄγωγ᾽ ἄρ᾽ οὐκ ἔθνησκον οὗ μ᾽ ἐχρῆν θανεῖν,
οὐδ᾽ ὤλεσέν με Ζεύς, τρέφει δ᾽, ὅπως ὁρῶ
κακῶν κάκ᾽ ἄλλα μείζον᾽ ἡ τάλαιν᾽ ἐγώ.
εἰ δ᾽ ἔστι τοῖς δούλοισι τοὺς ἐλευθέρους
μὴ λυπρὰ μηδὲ καρδίας δηκτήρια   235
ἐξιστορῆσαι, σοὶ μὲν εἰρῆσθαι χρεών,
ἡμᾶς δ᾽ ἀκοῦσαι τοὺς ἐρωτῶντας τάδε.

Οδ. ἔξεστ᾽, ἐρώτα· τοῦ χρόνου γὰρ οὐ φθονῶ.
Εκ. οἶσθ᾽ ἡνίκ᾽ ἦλθες Ἰλίου κατάσκοπος,
δυσχλαινίᾳ τ᾽ ἄμορφος, ὀμμάτων τ᾽ ἄπο   240
φόνου σταλαγμοὶ σὴν κατέσταζον γένυν ;
Οδ. οἶδ᾽· οὐ γὰρ ἄκρας καρδίας ἔψαυσέ μου.
Εκ. ἔγνω δέ σ᾽ Ἑλένη καὶ μόνῃ κατεῖπ᾽ ἐμοί ;
Οδ. μεμνήμεθ᾽ ἐς κίνδυνον ἐλθόντες μέγαν.
Εκ. ἥψω δὲ γονάτων τῶν ἐμῶν ταπεινὸς ὤν ;   245
Οδ. ὥστ᾽ ἐνθανεῖν γε σοῖς πέπλοισι χεῖρ᾽ ἐμήν.
Εκ. ἔσωσα δῆτά σ᾽ ἐξέπεμψά τε χθονός ;
Οδ. ὥστ᾽ εἰσορᾶν γε φέγγος ἡλίου τόδε.
Εκ. τί δῆτ᾽ ἔλεξας δοῦλος ὢν ἐμὸς τότε ;
Οδ. πολλῶν λόγων εὑρήμαθ᾽, ὥστε μὴ θανεῖν.   250

Hecuba. Would not this policy, then, prove your baseness,
　　Owing this debt, as you confess you owe it,
　　To pay me with no good, but your worst ill?
　　　O thankless brood, who jostle to be called
　　The people's leaders, may I not even know you!　255
　　Who turn a phrase to catch the mob's applause,
　　And care not if your phrase destroy your friend.
　　　And yet... what subtle reason can have swayed them
　　To cast their votes for death, and this child's death?
　　Necessity?　No, the tomb's fit sacrifice　260
　　Is blood of cattle slain, not human murder.
　　Or was it Justice?　Doth Achilles claim
　　Vengeance from those who slew him, life for life?
　　Why aim the shaft at her?　How has she wronged
　　　him?
　　Helen's the life he should have claimed, for Helen　265
　　Destroyed him, when she made him sail to Troy.
　　You have no fairer captive, and no prize
　　Of beauty fitter for the sacrifice:
　　No Trojan maid is half so fair as she,
　　And none has done you greater injury.　270
　　　Such is my plea if Justice judge between us.
　　But I have yet to tell you of a debt
　　Due to me when I claim it.　You have said,
　　You took my hand, you touched my cheek, and
　　　prayed:
　　So now I pray to you; I touch your hand　275
　　And cheek, and for the mercy shown you, claim
　　This kindness—Do not take my child from me
　　And kill her.　Are there not dead enough already?
　　She is my joy, my sweet forgetfulness　280
　　Of grief, my consolation for much loss,
　　My country and my nurse, my staff, my guide...
　　　The mighty should not use their might for evil,
　　Nor think, if Fortune smiles, they still must thrive
　　For ever.　I was Hecuba.　I am nothing—
　　All that prosperity snatched from me in a day.　285

[*She grasps his hand and touches his beard in the ritual
of supplication.*]

ἀλλ', ὦ φίλον γένειον, αἰδέσθητί με,
οἴκτιρον· ἐλθὼν δ' εἰς Ἀχαιικὸν στρατὸν

παρηγόρησον, ὡς ἀποκτείνειν φθόνος
γυναῖκας, ἃς τὸ πρῶτον οὐκ ἐκτείνατε
βωμῶν ἀποσπάσαντες, ἀλλ' ᾠκτίρατε.   290
νόμος δ' ἐν ὑμῖν τοῖς τ' ἐλευθέροις ἴσος
καὶ τοῖσι δούλοις αἵματος κεῖται πέρι.
τὸ δ' ἀξίωμα, κἂν κακῶς λέγῃ, τὸ σὸν
πείσει· λόγος γὰρ ἔκ τ' ἀδοξούντων ἰὼν
κἀκ τῶν δοκούντων αὐτὸς οὐ ταὐτὸν σθένει.   295

Χο. οὐκ ἔστιν οὕτω στερρὸς ἀνθρώπου φύσις,
ἥτις γόων σῶν καὶ μακρῶν ὀδυρμάτων
κλύουσα θρήνους οὐκ ἂν ἐκβάλοι δάκρυ.

Οδ. Ἑκάβη, διδάσκου, μηδὲ τῷ θυμουμένῳ
τὸν εὖ λέγοντα δυσμενῆ ποιοῦ φρενός.   300
ἐγὼ τὸ μὲν σὸν σῶμ' ὑφ' οὗπερ εὐτύχουν
σῴζειν ἕτοιμός εἰμι κοὐκ ἄλλως λέγω·
ἃ δ' εἶπον εἰς ἅπαντας οὐκ ἀρνήσομαι,
Τροίας ἁλούσης ἀνδρὶ τῷ πρώτῳ στρατοῦ
σὴν παῖδα δοῦναι σφάγιον ἐξαιτουμένῳ.   305
ἐν τῷδε γὰρ κάμνουσιν αἱ πολλαὶ πόλεις,
ὅταν τις ἐσθλὸς καὶ πρόθυμος ὢν ἀνὴρ
μηδὲν φέρηται τῶν κακιόνων πλέον.
ἡμῖν δ' Ἀχιλλεὺς ἄξιος τιμῆς, γύναι,
θανὼν ὑπὲρ γῆς Ἑλλάδος κάλλιστ' ἀνήρ.   310
οὔκουν τόδ' αἰσχρόν, εἰ βλέποντι μὲν φίλῳ
χρώμεσθ', ἐπεὶ δ' ὄλωλε, μὴ χρώμεσθ' ἔτι;
εἶεν· τί δῆτ' ἐρεῖ τις, ἤν τις αὖ φανῇ
στρατοῦ τ' ἄθροισις πολεμίων τ' ἀγωνία;
πότερα μαχούμεθ' ἢ φιλοψυχήσομεν,   315
τὸν κατθανόνθ' ὁρῶντες οὐ τιμώμενον;

For my part, in my life, a modest portion,
Enough from day to day, could well content me;
But after death I covet for my tomb
Honour, that lives when other joys are done.   320
    You tell me of your sorrows.   You shall hear
My answer.   We have women old as you

And not a jot less wretched; old men too,
And young brides widowed of the gallant men
Whose bones lie buried on your Trojan hills.　325
Bear, then, your griefs, as we will bear our folly,
If we *be* fools to honour heroes thus :—
Is it your foreign custom to forget
Your friends, and grudge the noble dead their praise?
Maintain it so, that Greece may prosper still,　330
And you, whose ways are evil, suffer ill.

Chorus. Oh misery of bondage, by the strong
Still driven, still constrained to suffer wrong!

[*Throughout this dialogue* POLYXENA *has been standing silent in the centre of the tableau.* HECUBA *now addresses her.*]

Hecuba. My daughter, pleading for your life, in vain
I spend my words upon the idle air.　335
If you have any skill your mother lacks,
Be zealous. Like the eloquent nightingale,
Thrilling her various woes, clamour for life.
Bend low for mercy at Odysseus' knee,
And plead—You have your argument. He too　340
Has children. Surely he must pity you.

Polyxena. I see, Odysseus, how you hide your hand
And turn away your head, for fear that I
May touch your cheek. Have courage. You are
safe.　345
I'll not invoke the suppliant's god, but go,
Willingly, yielding to necessity,
Because I wish to die, and not to wish it
Would prove a base ignoble love of life.

τί γάρ με δεῖ ζῆν; ἢ πατὴρ μὲν ἦν ἄναξ
Φρυγῶν ἁπάντων· τοῦτό μοι πρῶτον βίου·　350
ἔπειτ' ἐθρέφθην ἐλπίδων καλῶν ὕπο
βασιλεῦσι νύμφη, ζῆλον οὐ σμικρὸν γάμων
ἔχουσ', ὅτου δῶμ' ἑστίαν τ' ἀφίξομαι·
δέσποινα δ' ἡ δύστηνος 'Ιδαίαισιν ἢ
γυναιξὶ παρθένοις τ' ἀπόβλεπτος μέτα,　355
ἴση θεοῖσι πλὴν τὸ κατθανεῖν μόνον·

νῦν δ' εἰμὶ δούλη.   πρῶτα μέν με τοὔνομα
θανεῖν ἐρᾶν τίθησιν οὐκ εἰωθὸς ὄν·
ἔπειτ' ἴσως ἂν δεσποτῶν ὠμῶν φρένας
τύχοιμ' ἄν, ὅστις ἀργύρου μ' ὠνήσεται,   360
τὴν Ἕκτορός τε χἀτέρων πολλῶν κάσιν,
προσθεὶς δ' ἀνάγκην σιτοποιὸν ἐν δόμοις,
σαίρειν τε δῶμα κερκίσιν τ' ἐφεστάναι
λυπρὰν ἄγουσαν ἡμέραν μ' ἀναγκάσει·
λέχη δὲ τἀμὰ δοῦλος ὠνητός ποθεν   365
χρανεῖ, τυράννων πρόσθεν ἠξιωμένα.
οὐ δῆτ'· ἀφίημ' ὀμμάτων ἐλεύθερον
φέγγος τόδ', Ἀίδῃ προστιθεῖσ' ἐμὸν δέμας.
ἄγου μ', Ὀδυσσεῦ, καὶ διέργασαί μ' ἄγων·
οὔτ' ἐλπίδος γὰρ οὔτε του δόξης ὁρῶ   370
θάρσος παρ' ἡμῖν ὥς ποτ' εὖ πρᾶξαί με χρή.
μῆτερ, σὺ δ' ἡμῖν μηδὲν ἐμποδὼν γένῃ,
λέγουσα μηδὲ δρῶσα· συμβούλου δέ μοι
θανεῖν πρὶν αἰσχρῶν μὴ κατ' ἀξίαν τυχεῖν.
ὅστις γὰρ οὐκ εἴωθε γεύεσθαι κακῶν,   375
φέρει μέν, ἀλγεῖ δ' αὐχέν' ἐντιθεὶς ζυγῷ·
θανὼν δ' ἂν εἴη μᾶλλον εὐτυχέστερος
ἢ ζῶν· τὸ γὰρ ζῆν μὴ καλῶς μέγας πόνος.

Chorus. It is a mystery, yet it is manifest,
      The print of birth : and true nobility   380
      Shows nobler than its name when joined with honour.
Hecuba. Daughter, your words are brave, but in their
            virtue
      Is grief for me.   If you must sacrifice
      To appease the son of Peleus and be quit
      Of his reproach, make not the child your victim,   385
      Odysseus.   Here am I.   At Achilles' tomb
      Strike, do not spare me.   Paris was my son,
      And by his arrow Thetis' son was killed.
Odysseus. No, ancient mother.   It was not your death
      Achilles' shade demanded, but the maid's.   390
Hecuba. Kill me at least with her : so shall the earth

And he who craves of you this sacrifice
Receive a double offering of blood.
Odysseus. The maiden's death suffices. We'll not add
Bloodshed to bloodshed. Would that she, too, might
   live. 395
Hecuba. You needs must slay me. I will die with her.
Odysseus. Must, must? I know no master to command
   me.
Hecuba. As ivy to the oak, I will cling to her.
Odysseus. If you are well advised, madam, you will not.
Hecuba. I will not give her up. You shall not take
   her. 400
Odysseus. Madam, be sure I shall not go without her.

Polyxena. Mother, be ruled by me . . . Gently, Odysseus!
Her passion is not strange. She is my mother . . .
They are too strong for you. Give up the struggle,
Or they will lay rough hands on you, and seize 405
In their strong arms your venerable body—
Madam, they would . . . It is not fit they should!
And fling it to the ground, shamed and abused . . .
   Mother, sweet mother, give me your dear hand.
Touch my face. Closer! Lay your cheek to mine
   . . . 410
So, for the last time, never any more,
Greeting the orbéd splendour of the sun,
With these last words that ever I shall say,
My mother, out of life I go my way.
Hecuba. And leave me living, in the light, a slave! 415
Polyxena. Unwedded, I that should have been a bride!
Hecuba. 'Tis pity, child. Yet I was the bride of sorrow.
Polyxena. And I, so far from you, mother, in Hades.
Hecuba. Alas, what shall I do? Where ends my story?
Polyxena. I was born a free man's child. I die a slave.
Hecuba. I have borne fifty children. I die childless. 420
Polyxena. Have you some word for Priam, or for Hector?
Hecuba. This, that there is no sorrow like my sorrow.

Πλ. ὦ στέρνα μαστοί θ', οἵ μ' ἐθρέψαθ' ἡδέως.
Εκ. ὦ τῆς ἀώρου θύγατερ ἀθλία τύχης. 425
Πλ. χαῖρ', ὦ τεκοῦσα, χαῖρε Κασάνδρα τ' ἐμοί,
Εκ. χαίρουσιν ἄλλοι, μητρὶ δ' οὐκ ἔστιν τόδε.

Πλ. ὅ τ' ἐν φιλίπποις Θρῃξὶ Πολύδωρος κάσις.

Εκ. εἰ ζῇ γ'· ἀπιστῶ δ'· ὧδε πάντα δυστυχῶ.

Πλ. ζῇ καὶ θανούσης ὄμμα συγκλῄσει τὸ σόν.   430

Εκ. τέθνηκ' ἔγωγε πρὶν θανεῖν κακῶν ὕπο.

Πλ. κόμιζ', Ὀδυσσεῦ, μ' ἀμφιθεὶς κάρα πέπλοις
    ὡς πρὶν σφαγῆναί γ' ἐκτέτηκα καρδίαν
    θρήνοισι μητρὸς τήνδε τ' ἐκτήκω γόοις.
    ὦ φῶς· προσειπεῖν γὰρ σὸν ὄνομ' ἔξεστί μοι,   435
    μέτεστι δ' οὐδὲν πλὴν ὅσον χρόνον ξίφους
    βαίνω μεταξὺ καὶ πυρᾶς Ἀχιλλέως.

Εκ. οἲ 'γώ, προλείπω· λύεται δέ μου μέλη.
    ὦ θύγατερ, ἅψαι μητρός, ἔκτεινον χέρα,
    δός· μὴ λίπῃς μ' ἄπαιδ'. ἀπωλόμην, φίλαι. . . . 440

[*During these words* POLYXENA, *veiled, is led away by*
ODYSSEUS. HECUBA *rouses herself to a last effort, prays
for vengeance on* HELEN, *then collapses.*]

    ὡς τὴν Λάκαιναν σύγγονον Διοσκόροιν
    Ἑλένην ἴδοιμι· διὰ καλῶν γὰρ ὀμμάτων
    αἴσχιστα Τροίαν εἷλε τὴν εὐδαίμονα.

Χο.—   αὔρα, ποντιὰς αὔρα,   [στρ.
       ἅτε ποντοπόρους κομί-   445
    ζεις θοὰς ἀκάτους ἐπ' οἶδμα λίμνας,
       ποῖ με τὰν μελέαν πορεύ-
       σεις; τῷ δουλόσυνος πρὸς οἶ-
       κον κτηθεῖσ' ἀφίξομαι; ἢ
          Δωρίδος ὅρμον αἴας;   450
    ἢ Φθιάδος, ἔνθα τὸν
    καλλίστων ὑδάτων πατέρα
    φασὶν Ἀπιδανὸν πεδία λιπαίνειν;

    Or perchance to an island   *Antistr.* 1
    Oars that beat for the land shall bring me,
        Alas, to a life, a home of sorrow,
          Delos, home of the palm and laurel   456
        That sprang to the light and flourished

For Leto's Majesty
And grace of the holy travail :   460
  Ah, shall it be mine to praise
Artemis, and her golden crown
And her archery, with the maids of Delos ?

  O City that Pallas loves,   *Str.* 2
  Great goddess of horse and car !
There perchance I shall weave for thee
Raiment of saffron hue,
Pictured steeds and a web of wondrous flowers, broidered
    about with beauty ;
Or those sons of the Earth,   470
Whelmed by Zeus in the flame,
Titans, laid to rest by the God.

  ὤ μοι τεκέων ἐμῶν,   [ἀντ.
  ὤ μοι πατέρων χθονός θ',   476
 ἅ καπνῷ κατερείπεται,
 τυφομένα, δορίκτητος
Ἀργείων· ἐγὼ δ' ἐν ξεί-
να χθονὶ δὴ κέκλημαι δού-   480
   λα, λιποῦσ' Ἀσίαν,
Εὐρώπας θεράπναν ἀλλά-
   ξασ''Ἀιδα θαλάμους.

[*Enter* TALTHYBIUS, AGAMEMNON's *Herald.*]

ΤΑΛΘΥΒΙΟΣ
  ποῦ τὴν ἄνασσαν δή ποτ' οὖσαν Ἰλίου
  Ἑκάβην ἂν ἐξεύροιμι, Τρῳάδες κόραι ;   485
Χο. αὕτη πέλας σου νῶτ' ἔχουσ' ἐπὶ χθονί,
  Ταλθύβιε, κεῖται ξυγκεκλημένη πέπλοις.
Τα. ὦ Ζεῦ, τί λέξω ; πότερά σ' ἀνθρώπους ὁρᾶν ;
  ἢ δόξαν ἄλλως τήνδε κεκτῆσθαι μάτην,
  ψευδῆ, δοκοῦντας δαιμόνων εἶναι γένος   490
  τύχην δὲ πάντα τὰν βροτοῖς ἐπισκοπεῖν ;
  οὐχ ἥδ' ἄνασσα τῶν πολυχρύσων Φρυγῶν,
  οὐχ ἥδε Πριάμου τοῦ μέγ' ὀλβίου δάμαρ ;

καὶ νῦν πόλις μὲν πᾶσ' ἀνέστηκεν δορί,
αὐτὴ δὲ δούλη γραῦς ἄπαις ἐπὶ χθονὶ   495
κεῖται, κόνει φύρουσα δύστηνον κάρα.
φεῦ φεῦ· γέρων μὲν εἰμ', ὅμως δέ μοι θανεῖν
εἴη πρὶν αἰσχρᾷ περιπεσεῖν τύχῃ τινί.
    ἀνίστασ', ὦ δύστηνε, καὶ μετάρσιον
πλευρὰν ἔπαιρε καὶ τὸ πάλλευκον κάρα.   500

Hecuba. Why, who is this that will not leave my body
   In peace? Let grief lie still, whoe'er you are.
Talthybius. I am Talthybius. I serve the Greeks.
   I come for you by Agamemnon's order.
Hecuba. The Greeks? Oh, will they sacrifice me too? 505
   Then welcome, friend. You bring me welcome news.
   Let us make haste, old herald. Show me the way.
Talthybius. This is my message. I am instructed, madam,
   By the two princes and the Achaean people,
   To bid you come and bury your dead child.   510
Hecuba. Ah me, what will you say? You have not come
   To fetch me to my death? You bring sad news?
      They have taken you from me, child, and you are
         dead,
   And all my motherhood in you is gone.
   Come, how did you dispatch? With reverence 515
   And honour? Or, as if you killed a foe,
   With outrage? Tell me. Though you hurt me,
      speak.
Talthybius. You bid me take a double meed of tears,
   In pity for your daughter. At the tomb
   I wept, and weep again to tell the story.   520
      In full assembly all the Achaean host
   Met for your daughter's sacrifice at the tomb.
   Achilles' offspring led Polyxena
   By the hand to the mound's summit. I was near her,
   And with me was a chosen company   525
   Of the Greek youth, appointed to restrain
   The child, if she had struggled. First the son,
   Poured to the father from a cup of gold
   Brimming libation, bidding me, with a sign,
   Make silence in the whole Achaean host.   530

Thereat I stood in the midst of them, and spoke :
' Peace, peace, Achaeans.   Every voice be hushed
In silence.'   And the people all were still.

Then he prayed, 'Son of Peleus, and my sire,
Take these propitious offerings, whose power   535
Is strong to move the dead.   Come, come, and drink
The dark stream of the maid's pure blood, which I
And all the army give thee.   Be appeased,
And grant that with thy blessing we may loose
The bonds that hold our ships, and all of us
With good success come safely home from Troy.'   540
He spoke, the people answering with prayer,
Then took by the hilt his sword, with gold inlaid,
And, as he drew it, nodded to the youth
Of Argos, chosen for the task, to seize the maid ;   545
Which she perceiving, spoke to them these words :
'You men of Argos, who have sacked my city,
I die of my own will.   Let no one touch
My body.   See, I give my throat to the knife
Bravely.   I pray you, let me die unbound.   550
Leave me free.   I am royal.   I should blush
Among the dead to bear the name of slave.'

λαοὶ δ' ἐπερρόθησαν, Ἀγαμέμνων τ' ἄναξ
εἶπεν μεθεῖναι παρθένον νεανίαις.
οἳ δ', ὡς τάχιστ' ἤκουσαν ὑστάτην ὄπα,   555
μεθῆκαν, οὗπερ καὶ μέγιστον ἦν κράτος.
κἀπεὶ τόδ' εἰσήκουσε δεσποτῶν ἔπος,
λαβοῦσα πέπλους ἐξ ἄκρας ἐπωμίδος
ἔρρηξε λαγόνας ἐς μέσας παρ' ὀμφαλόν,
μαστούς τ' ἔδειξε στέρνα θ' ὡς ἀγάλματος   560
κάλλιστα, καὶ καθεῖσα πρὸς γαῖαν γόνυ
ἔλεξε πάντων τλημονέστατον λόγον·
Ἰδού, τόδ', εἰ μὲν στέρνον, ὦ νεανία,
παίειν προθυμῇ, παῖσον, εἰ δ' ὑπ' αὐχένα
χρῄζεις, πάρεστι λαιμὸς εὐτρεπὴς ὅδε.   565
ὃ δ' οὐ θέλων τε καὶ θέλων οἴκτῳ κόρης,
τέμνει σιδήρῳ πνεύματος διαρροάς·
κρουνοὶ δ' ἐχώρουν. ἣ δὲ καὶ θνῄσκουσ' ὅμως

πολλὴν πρόνοιαν εἶχεν εὐσχήμων πεσεῖν,
κρύπτουσ᾽ ἃ κρύπτειν ὄμματ᾽ ἀρσένων χρεών.   570
ἐπεὶ δ᾽ ἀφῆκε πνεῦμα θανασίμῳ σφαγῇ,
οὐδεὶς τὸν αὐτὸν εἶχεν Ἀργείων πόνον·
ἀλλ᾽ οἱ μὲν αὐτῶν τὴν θανοῦσαν ἐκ χερῶν
φύλλοις ἔβαλλον, οἱ δὲ πληροῦσιν πυρὰν
κορμοὺς φέροντες πευκίνους, ὁ δ᾽ οὐ φέρων   575
πρὸς τοῦ φέροντος τοιάδ᾽ ἤκουεν κακά·
Ἕστηκας, ὦ κάκιστε, τῇ νεάνιδι
οὐ πέπλον οὐδὲ κόσμον ἐν χεροῖν ἔχων ;
οὐκ εἶ τι δώσων τῇ περίσσ᾽ εὐκαρδίῳ
ψυχήν τ᾽ ἀρίστῃ ; τοιάδ᾽ ἀμφὶ σῆς λέγων   580
παιδὸς θανούσης· εὐτεκνωτάτην δέ σε
πασῶν γυναικῶν δυστυχεστάτην θ᾽ ὁρῶ.

Χο. δεινόν τι πῆμα Πριαμίδαις ἐπέζεσεν
     πόλει τε τῇ ῃ θεῶν ἀνάγκαισιν τόδε.

Εκ. ὦ θύγατερ, οὐκ οἶδ᾽ εἰς ὅ τι βλέψω κακῶν,   585
     πολλῶν παρόντων· ἢν γὰρ ἅψωμαί τινος,
     τόδ᾽ οὐκ ἐᾷ με, παρακαλεῖ δ᾽ ἐκεῖθεν αὖ
     λύπη τις ἄλλη διάδοχος κακῶν κακοῖς.

And this that you have suffered, though I weep—
I cannot so forget as not to weep—
Yet you have robbed grief of its sting, because   590
They say that you were noble. This is strange:
If the gods bless the season, the worst land
Bears a good harvest, and the fruitful soil,   595
Lacking due nurture, fails: it is not so
With us; with us, the bad are always bad,
And the good, good in nature, still unchanged
Though fortune changes, keep their virtue still.
And what's the secret? Is it birth? Or breeding?
Certainly, to be bred in a good habit   600
Teaches them honour, gives a rule, a standard,
By which to judge what's base . . . Alack! My mind
Is like an archer, shooting aimlessly.
     Go, tell the Greeks. Let no one touch my child;
Hold back the people. Multitudes in arms   605

Run violent, and a fleet grown riotous
Is swept by passion stronger than the flame
Of fire, and counts it crime to do no wrong.
   And you, old serving-woman, take a vessel,
And fill it with sea-water. I must wash 610
For the last time the body of this bride
That is no bride, this maid no more a maid,
And make her ready—not as she deserves—
Oh no, I could not—but as best I can.
For what resource have I? I'll gather up 615
Such treasures as the women lodged with me,
My fellow-slaves, have rescued from their homes
And kept, like thieves, from the new master's eye.

ὦ σχήματ' οἴκων, ὦ ποτ' εὐτυχεῖς δόμοι,
ὦ πλεῖστ' ἔχων κάλλιστά τ', εὐτεκνώτατε 620
Πρίαμε, γεραιά θ' ἥδ' ἐγὼ μήτηρ τέκνων,
ὡς ἐς τὸ μηδὲν ἥκομεν, φρονήματος
τοῦ πρὶν στερέντες.   εἶτα δῆτ' ὀγκούμεθα,
ὃ μέν τις ἡμῶν πλουσίοις ἐν δώμασιν,
ὃ δ' ἐν πολίταις τίμιος κεκλημένος. 625
τὰ δ' οὐδὲν ἄλλως, φροντίδων βουλεύματα
γλώσσης τε κόμποι.   κεῖνος ὀλβιώτατος,
ὅτῳ κατ' ἦμαρ τυγχάνει μηδὲν κακόν.

Χο.   ἐμοὶ χρῆν συμφοράν,   [στρ.
        ἐμοὶ χρῆν πημονὰν γενέσθαι, 630
      Ἰδαίαν ὅτε πρῶτον ὕλαν
      Ἀλέξανδρος εἰλατίναν
      ἐτάμεθ', ἅλιον ἐπ' οἶδμα ναυστολήσων
      Ἑλένας ἐπὶ λέκτρα, τὰν 635
        καλλίσταν ὁ χρυσοφαὴς
         Ἅλιος αὐγάζει.

  The wheel moves on, and brings,   *Antistr.*
    With labour, sorrow worse than labour. 640
One man sinned, but the fruits of madness,
    Destruction, a desolate land,
An irreparable woe, the people suffers.

For the end of the strife of Ida, when three great goddesses
        strove,   645
        Bidding a herdsman judge,

Is agony of death and war, and, alas, for me it is home laid
        low.
And there is mourning too on the banks of the fair broad
        stream
     Eurotas ; there is a weeping Spartan maid,   650
      And a mother of Sparta, grieving ;
     She weeps her children, and she tears her hair,
      And her cheeks with the traces   655
    Of bloodily disfiguring nails are furrowed.

[*The* SERVING-WOMAN *returns, bearing the body of*
POLYDORUS.]

Serving-Woman. Where is the queen of sorrow ?   Where
    is she
    Whose crown of grief surpasses all that man
    Or womankind have suffered ? Where is Hecuba ? 660
Chorus. Wretch, will you never let affliction sleep,
    But still cry out ?   Cease your ill-omened clamour.
Serving-Woman. It is not easy to find out good words
    For woe.   See, I bring pain for Hecuba.
Chorus. She is coming from her lodging, see ! Your
    tale   665
    Will not have long to wait.   She comes to meet it.
Serving-Woman. Sad mistress, sadder than my words can
    tell,
    Desolate, doomed to life that is no life,
    Husbandless, cityless, childless—all are taken.
Hecuba. This is no news, and you insult a grief   670
    With which we are acquainted.

[*She sees the body.*]

                   Why do you bring
    Polyxena's body here ?   The host, they said,
    Were all preparing for her burial.
Serving-Woman. She does not know.   She mourns Poly-
    xena,
    And does not feel the touch of this new sorrow.   675
Hecuba. Ah, woe is me !   Is it the sacred body
    Of my distraught Cassandra that you bring me ?

Serving-Woman. Your cry is for the living, not for him
    That's dead. Remove the veils. Look. Is not this
    A sight for wonder, past all expectation?   680
Hecuba. Ah!
    It is my son I see, and he is dead . . .
    Polydorus, who was safe . . . safe with the Thracian . . .
    I am lost, quite lost. I am no longer I.
        O my child! My child!
    Alas, what mean these frenzied strains?   685
    What fiend of vengeance maddens me,
      When I would sing thy dirge?
Serving-Woman. Poor soul, you know it now. Your son
    is dead!
Hecuba.   Horror on horror, past imagination,
    Oh, it is past belief! And yet I see it,   690
    And never a day shall come when I shall cease my
      weeping,
    Or be at peace from sorrow.

Χο. δείν', ὦ τάλαινα, δεινὰ πάσχομεν κακά.
Εκ.   ὦ τέκνον τέκνον ταλαίνας ματρός,
    τίνι μόρῳ θνῄσκεις,   695
    τίνι πότμῳ κεῖσαι;
    πρὸς τίνος ἀνθρώπων;
Θε.   οὐκ οἶδ'· ἐπ' ἀκταῖς νιν κυρῶ θαλασσίαις . . .
Εκ.   ἔκβλητον, ἢ πέσημα φοινίου δορός,
    ἐν ψαμάθῳ λευρᾷ;   700
Θε.   πόντου νιν ἐξήνεγκε πελάγιος κλύδων.
Εκ.   ὤμοι, αἰαῖ, ἔμαθον ἔνυπνον ὀμμάτων
    ἐμῶν ὄψιν· οὔ με παρέβα
    φάσμα μελανόπτερον, τὰν ἐσεῖδον ἀμφὶ σέ,   705
    ὦ τέκνον, οὐκέτ' ὄντα Διὸς ἐν φάει.
Χο. τίς γάρ νιν ἔκτειν'; οἶσθ' ὀνειρόφρων φράσαι;
Εκ.   ἐμὸς ἐμὸς ξένος, Θρήκιος ἱππότας,   710
    ἵν' ὁ γέρων πατὴρ ἔθετό νιν κρύψας.
Χο. οἴμοι, τί λέξεις; χρυσὸν ὡς ἔχοι κτανών;
Εκ. ἄρρητ' ἀνωνόμαστα, θαυμάτων πέρα,
    οὐχ ὅσι' οὐδ' ἀνεκτά. ποῦ δίκα ξένων;   715

ὦ κατάρατ' ἀνδρῶν, ὡς διεμοιράσω
χρόα, σιδαρέῳ τεμὼν φασγάνῳ
μέλεα τοῦδε παιδὸς οὐδ' ᾤκτισας.   720

[*Enter* AGAMEMNON, *attended.* HECUBA *remains crouching
over the body, with her face towards the audience.*]

Χο. ὦ τλῆμον, ὥς σε πολυπονωτάτην βροτῶν
δαίμων ἔθηκεν ὅστις ἐστί σοι βαρύς.
ἀλλ' εἰσορῶ γὰρ τοῦδε δεσπότου δέμας
Ἀγαμέμνονος, τοὐνθένδε σιγῶμεν, φίλαι.   725

ΑΓΑΜΕΜΝΩΝ

Ἑκάβη, τί μέλλεις παῖδα σὴν κρύπτειν τάφῳ
ἐλθοῦσ', ἐφ' οἷσπερ Ταλθύβιος ἤγγειλέ μοι
μὴ θιγγάνειν σῆς μηδέν' Ἀργείων κόρης;
ἡμεῖς μὲν οὖν εἰῶμεν οὐδ' ἐψαύομεν·
σὺ δὲ σχολάζεις, ὥστε θαυμάζειν ἐμέ.   730
ἥκω δ' ἀποστελῶν σε· τἀκεῖθεν γὰρ εὖ
πεπραγμέν' ἐστίν—εἴ τι τῶνδ' ἐστὶν καλῶς.
    ἔα· τίν' ἄνδρα τόνδ' ἐπὶ σκηναῖς ὁρῶ
θανόντα Τρώων; οὐ γὰρ Ἀργεῖον πέπλοι
δέμας περιπτύσσοντες ἀγγέλλουσί μοι.   735

Hecuba [*aside*]. O wretched; for the name of wretchedness
Is Hecuba's name; what shall I do? Implore
His help? Or suffer all my wrongs in silence?
Agamemnon. Why do you turn away and weep, and say
No word of what has happened? Who is this?   740
Hecuba. What if he spurn me from him as his slave
And enemy? I should but court fresh sorrow.
Agamemnon. I have no skill in divination.
I cannot read your thoughts unless you speak.
Hecuba. My thoughts? Am I too quick to read in him   745
Enmity, where there is no enmity?
Agamemnon. You wish me to know nothing? We are one
In that desire. I have no wish to know.
Hecuba. Without this man I cannot hope to win   750
My vengeance for my child. Why hesitate?
Venture I must, whether I win or lose.

[*She suddenly rises and flings herself at his knee.*]

Agamemnon, I am your suppliant.   By your knees
I pray, and beard, and prosperous right hand.

Agamemnon. What is it you would have of me ?   A life   755
Of freedom ?   You may have it readily.

Hecuba. No, no, I am content to be a slave
If I may have vengeance upon the wicked.

Agamemnon. Why, what is this ?   How would you have
us help you ?

Hecuba. It is not in your thoughts, my lord.   You see
This body, and you see me weep for it.   760

Agamemnon. I see, but I have still to read the meaning.

Hecuba. This was my child, a son born of my womb.

Agamemnon. Alas, which of your children, sorrowful one ?

Hecuba. Not one of Priam's sons who fell at Troy.

Agamemnon. Had you another son, madam, besides ?   765

Hecuba. Yes.   This is he.   I have no joy of him.

Agamemnon. Where was he when destruction came to
Troy ?

Hecuba. His father feared for his life and sent him out—

Agamemnon. Yes, yes, one child of his house—where did
he send him ?

Hecuba. Here, to this country, where we find him,
dead.   770

Agamemnon. To Polymestor ?   To the Prince of Thrace ?

Hecuba. To him . . . with a fatal treasure-store of gold.

Agamemnon. How did he come to die ?   Who caused his
death ?

Hecuba. Who else ?   It is his Thracian host, has killed
him.

Agamemnon. An outrage . . . Was he lured by the lust of
the gold ?   775

Hecuba. Surely, when once he knew that we were helpless.

Agamemnon. Where was the body found ?   Who brought
it you ?

Hecuba. On the sea-shore.   My serving-woman found him.

Agamemnon. Why did you send her there ?   To search
for the body ?

Hecuba. No, to fetch lustral water . . . for Polyxena.   780

Agamemnon [*after a pause*]. So then, he killed his friend,
and cast him out . . .

Hecuba. To drift in the waves, a mutilated body.

Agamemnon. O tragic heart, O grief, past measuring . . .
Hecuba. Lost, Agamemnon : nothing left to suffer.

Αγ. φεῦ φεῦ· τίς οὕτω δυστυχὴς ἔφυ γυνή;   785
Εκ. οὐκ ἔστιν, εἰ μὴ τὴν Τύχην αὐτὴν λέγοις.

     ἀλλ᾽ ὧνπερ οὕνεκ᾽ ἀμφὶ σὸν πίπτω γόνυ
ἄκουσον. εἰ μὲν ὅσιά σοι παθεῖν δοκῶ,
στέργοιμ᾽ ἄν· εἰ δὲ τοὔμπαλιν, σύ μοι γενοῦ
τιμωρὸς ἀνδρός, ἀνοσιωτάτου ξένου,   790
ὃς οὔτε τοὺς γῆς νέρθεν οὔτε τοὺς ἄνω
δείσας δέδρακεν ἔργον ἀνοσιώτατον,
κοινῆς τραπέζης πολλάκις τυχὼν ἐμοί,
ξενίας τ᾽ ἀριθμῷ πρῶτ᾽ ἔχων ἐμῶν φίλων,
τυχὼν δ᾽ ὅσων δεῖ—. καὶ λαβὼν προμηθίαν   795
ἔκτεινε· τύμβου δ᾽, εἰ κτανεῖν ἐβούλετο,
οὐκ ἠξίωσεν, ἀλλ᾽ ἀφῆκε πόντιον.
ἡμεῖς μὲν οὖν δοῦλοί τε κἀσθενεῖς ἴσως·
ἀλλ᾽ οἱ θεοὶ σθένουσι χὠ κείνων κρατῶν
Νόμος· νόμῳ γὰρ τοὺς θεοὺς ἡγούμεθα   800
καὶ ζῶμεν ἄδικα καὶ δίκαι᾽ ὡρισμένοι·
ὃς ἐς σ᾽ ἀνελθὼν εἰ διαφθαρήσεται,
καὶ μὴ δίκην δώσουσιν οἵτινες ξένους
κτείνουσιν ἢ θεῶν ἱερὰ τολμῶσιν φέρειν,
οὐκ ἔστιν οὐδὲν τῶν ἐν ἀνθρώποις ἴσον.   805
ταῦτ᾽ οὖν ἐν αἰσχρῷ θέμενος αἰδέσθητί με·
οἴκτιρον ἡμᾶς, ὡς γραφεύς τ᾽ ἀποσταθεὶς
ἰδοῦ με κἀνάθρησον οἷ᾽ ἔχω κακά.
τύραννος ἦ ποτ᾽, ἀλλὰ νῦν δούλη σέθεν,
εὔπαις ποτ᾽ οὖσα, νῦν δὲ γραῦς ἄπαις θ᾽ ἅμα,   810
ἄπολις ἔρημος, ἀθλιωτάτη βροτῶν . . .

     οἴμοι τάλαινα, ποῖ μ᾽ ὑπεξάγεις πόδα;
ἔοικα πράξειν οὐδέν· ὦ τάλαιν᾽ ἐγώ.
τί δῆτα θνητοὶ τἄλλα μὲν μαθήματα
μοχθοῦμεν ὡς χρὴ πάντα καὶ ματεύομεν,   815
Πειθὼ δὲ τὴν τύραννον ἀνθρώποις μόνην
οὐδέν τι μᾶλλον ἐς τέλος σπουδάζομεν

μισθοὺς διδόντες μανθάνειν, ἵν' ἦν ποτε
πείθειν ἅ τις βούλοιτο τυγχάνειν θ' ἅμα;
πῶς οὖν ἔτ' ἄν τις ἐλπίσαι πράξειν καλῶς;   820
οἱ μὲν γὰρ ὄντες παῖδες οὐκέτ' εἰσί μοι,
αὕτη δ' ἐπ' αἰσχροῖς αἰχμάλωτος. οἴχομαι·
καπνὸν δὲ πόλεως τόνδ' ὑπερθρῴσκονθ' ὁρῶ.

And yet . . . it is a vanity perhaps
To speak of Love . . . and yet . . . This I will
    say . . .   825
My daughter, the prophetic maid, once known
In Phrygia as Cassandra, shares your bed.
How will you prove your happiness, my lord,
Or how requite her gift of dear embracements
With favour?   And what recompense is mine?   830

        .   .   .   .   .

        .   .   .   .   .

Then listen!   Look on him who here lies dead.
He is your kinsman.   Serving him, you serve
Your brother.   Why, here's yet some argument   835
Omitted . . . O for the craft of Daedalus
Or some kind god to fill with eloquence
Arms, hair and hands and feet, that all at once
Might cling about your knees, and cry their grief,
And leave no word unspoken, and prevail . . .   840
    My Lord, my Master, Light of the Day of Greece,
Lift up your hand in vengeance: I am old,
And I am come to nothing: yet avenge!
This, this is virtue: to do justice still,
Requiting evil every way with ill.   845
Chorus. See how the fates of mortal men are linked
    By nature's law in strange affinities,
    And harshest enemies by circumstance
    Are turned to friends, and friends to enemies.
Agamemnon. Yourself, your son, and your calamity, 850
    And these your prayers, I pity, Hecuba;
    And wish, in the cause of justice and religion,
    You might have vengeance on this infamous friend,
    If I could give you satisfaction, free
    From all suspicion of my soldiery
    That I destroyed him for Cassandra's sake.   855

I am perplexed.   The Prince of Thrace is ranked
By the army as a friend, and your dead son
A Trojan enemy.   Is he near to me
In kinship now?   That is a private bond ;   860
Nothing to them.   Think well.   You have in me
A willing helper, eager in your cause,
But slow to court the censure of the army.

Εκ.   φεῦ.
 οὐκ ἔστι θνητῶν ὅστις ἔστ᾽ ἐλεύθερος·
 ἢ χρημάτων γὰρ δοῦλός ἐστιν ἢ τύχης,   865
 ἢ πλῆθος αὐτὸν πόλεος ἢ νόμων γραφαὶ
 εἴργουσι χρῆσθαι μὴ κατὰ γνώμην τρόποις.
 ἐπεὶ δὲ ταρβεῖς τῷ τ᾽ ὄχλῳ πλέον νέμεις,
 ἐγώ σε θήσω τοῦδ᾽ ἐλεύθερον φόβου.
 σύνισθι μὲν γάρ, ἤν τι βουλεύσω κακὸν   870
 τῷ τόνδ᾽ ἀποκτείναντι, συνδράσῃς δὲ μή.
 ἢν δ᾽ ἐξ Ἀχαιῶν θόρυβος ἢ ᾽πικουρία
 πάσχοντος ἀνδρὸς Θρῃκὸς οἷα πείσεται
 φανῇ τις, εἶργε μὴ δοκῶν ἐμὴν χάριν.
 τὰ δ᾽ ἄλλα—θάρσει—πάντ᾽ ἐγὼ θήσω καλῶς.   875
Αγ.   πῶς οὖν ; τί δράσεις ; πότερα φάσγανον χερὶ
 λαβοῦσα γραίᾳ φῶτα βάρβαρον κτενεῖς,
 ἢ φαρμάκοισιν ἢ ᾽πικουρίᾳ τινί ;
 τίς σοι ξυνέσται χείρ ; πόθεν κτήσῃ φίλους ;
Εκ.   στέγαι κεκεύθασ᾽ αἵδε Τρῳάδων ὄχλον.   880
Αγ.   τὰς αἰχμαλώτους εἶπας, Ἑλλήνων ἄγραν ;
Εκ.   σὺν ταῖσδε τὸν ἐμὸν φονέα τιμωρήσομαι.
Αγ.   καὶ πῶς γυναιξὶν ἀρσένων ἔσται κράτος ;
Εκ.   δεινὸν τὸ πλῆθος σὺν δόλῳ τε δύσμαχον.
Αγ.   δεινόν· τὸ μέντοι θῆλυ μέμφομαι γένος.   885
Εκ.   τί δ᾽; οὐ γυναῖκες εἷλον Αἰγύπτου τέκνα
 καὶ Λῆμνον ἄρδην ἀρσένων ἐξῴκισαν ;
 ἀλλ᾽ ὡς γενέσθω· τόνδε μὲν μέθες λόγον,
 πέμψον δέ μοι τήνδ᾽ ἀσφαλῶς διὰ στρατοῦ
 γυναῖκα.—

[*To the* SERVING-WOMAN.]

καὶ σὺ Θρῃκὶ πλαθεῖσα ξένῳ   890
λέξον· Καλεῖ σ' ἄνασσα δή ποτ' Ἰλίου
Ἑκάβη, σὸν οὐκ ἔλασσον ἢ κείνης χρέος,
καὶ παῖδας· ὡς δεῖ καὶ τέκν' εἰδέναι λόγους
τοὺς ἐξ ἐκείνης.—τὸν δὲ τῆς νεοσφαγοῦς
Πολυξένης ἐπίσχες, Ἀγάμεμνον, τάφον,   895
ὡς τώδ' ἀδελφὼ πλησίον μιᾷ φλογί,
δισσὴ μέριμνα μητρί, κρυφθῆτον χθονί.

Agamemnon. It shall be done.   I could not so indulge you,
     Had it been possible for the fleet to sail.
     But since God sends no favouring wind, we wait,   900
     And needs must wait, until the voyage be fair.
     May some good end it.   For it touches all,
     Cities and men alike, that deeds of ill
     Find evil ends, and virtue prosper still.

Chorus.

My fatherland, O my Troy!
None shall hail thee now, the impregnable city,   906
Shrouded, compassed round by the host of Hellas,
     By the spear of the spoiler.
     They have shorn from thy brow the beauty   910
     Thy towers.   We have seen thy ways
     Ravaged, smirched by the smoke of ruin,
          Alas!   Ways that are mine no longer.

In the night was my sorrow born,
When the feast was done, at the hour when the weary   915
Turn to sleep.   Ah sweet! when the song and the dancing
     And the worship were over,
     And my lord in the bower was waiting;
     His spear on the wall, at rest;
     No more watch at the ships, no longer   920
     Trampling feet in the Trojan city;

And I in ribands and laces caught
And twined the tresses of my hair,
     And read the dim glad secret   925
          The haze of my mirror told,

Of a bride and a happy lover, waiting . . .
    A stir in the city, and a noise,
A shout that rang in the streets of Troy,
      Crying, 'Up,
Sons of Grecian sires, it is time, it is time!   930
    Will ye not ravage and sack
      Troy's tower and turn you homeward?'

I left the bed of my lord, I ran,
In the shift of a Dorian maid, ungirt;
    I sought thy shrine, in vain;   935
      Goddess, Artemis! All in vain!
For they took me, they slew my lord, I saw him,
  My lord, and they dragged me to the sea
Still gazing back to Troy . . . The ship
    Homeward-bound
Strained her tackling eagerly, bearing me on   940
    Far from the land of my love,
      Ah grief! my spirit left me,

And, fainting, cried my curse upon Helen, my curse on
    fatal Paris—   945
Herdsman of Ida, and sister of the sons of Zeus.
    Torn from that ruined fatherland,
Outcast from home, I curse her, the bride who was not a
    bride, but a fiend, a fury,
And pray that the waves of the sea may not carry her again
    safe home,   950
      Never more
    Home, to her father's country.

[*Enter* POLYMESTOR, *Prince of Thrace, with the two princes,
    his sons, and bodyguard.*]

ΠΟΛΥΜΗΣΤΩΡ

    ὦ φίλτατ' ἀνδρῶν Πρίαμε, φιλτάτη δὲ σύ,
    Ἑκάβη, δακρύω σ' εἰσορῶν πόλιν τε σὴν
    τήν τ' ἀρτίως θανοῦσαν ἔκγονον σέθεν.   955
    φεῦ·
    οὐκ ἔστι πιστὸν οὐδέν, οὔτ' εὐδοξία
    οὔτ' αὖ καλῶς πράσσοντα μὴ πράξειν κακῶς.
    φύρουσι δ' αὐτοὶ θεοὶ πάλιν τε καὶ πρόσω

ταραγμὸν ἐντιθέντες, ὡς ἀγνωσίᾳ
σέβωμεν αὐτούς. ἀλλὰ ταῦτα μὲν τί δεῖ 960
θρηνεῖν, προκόπτοντ' οὐδὲν ἐς πρόσθεν κακῶν;
σὺ δ', εἴ τι μέμφῃ τῆς ἐμῆς ἀπουσίας,
σχές· τυγχάνω γὰρ ἐν μέσοις Θρῄκης ὅροις
ἀπών, ὅτ' ἦλθες δεῦρ'· ἐπεὶ δ' ἀφικόμην,
ἤδη πόδ' ἔξω δωμάτων αἴροντί μοι 965
ἐς ταὐτὸν ἥδε συμπίτνει δμωὶς σέθεν
λέγουσα μύθους, ὧν κλύων ἀφικόμην.
Εκ. αἰσχύνομαί σε προσβλέπειν ἐναντίον,
Πολυμῆστορ, ἐν τοιοῖσδε κειμένη κακοῖς.
ὅτῳ γὰρ ὤφθην εὐτυχοῦσ', αἰδώς μ' ἔχει 970
ἐν τῷδε πότμῳ τυγχάνουσ' ἵν' εἰμὶ νῦν
κοὐκ ἂν δυναίμην προσβλέπειν ὀρθαῖς κόραις.
ἀλλ' αὐτὸ μὴ δύσνοιαν ἡγήσῃ σέθεν,
Πολυμῆστορ· ἄλλως δ' αἴτιόν τι καὶ νόμος,
γυναῖκας ἀνδρῶν μὴ βλέπειν ἐναντίον. 975
Πλ. καὶ θαῦμά γ' οὐδέν. ἀλλὰ τίς χρεία σ' ἐμοῦ;
τί χρῆμ' ἐπέμψω τὸν ἐμὸν ἐκ δόμων πόδα·
Εκ. ἴδιον ἐμαυτῆς δή τι πρὸς σὲ βούλομαι
καὶ παῖδας εἰπεῖν σούς· ὀπάονας δέ μοι
χωρὶς κέλευσον τῶνδ' ἀποστῆναι δόμων. 980
Πλ. χωρεῖτ'· ἐν ἀσφαλεῖ γὰρ ἥδ' ἐρημία.

[The bodyguard withdraws]

φίλη μὲν εἶ σύ, προσφιλὲς δέ μοι τόδε
στράτευμ' Ἀχαιῶν. ἀλλὰ σημαίνειν σὲ χρῆν·
τί χρὴ τὸν εὖ πράσσοντα μὴ πράσσουσιν εὖ
φίλοις ἐπαρκεῖν; ὡς ἕτοιμός εἰμ' ἐγώ. 985
Εκ. πρῶτον μὲν εἰπὲ παῖδ' ὃν ἐξ ἐμῆς χερὸς
Πολύδωρον ἔκ τε πατρὸς ἐν δόμοις ἔχεις,
εἰ ζῇ· τὰ δ' ἄλλα δεύτερόν σ' ἐρήσομαι.
Πλ. μάλιστα· τοὐκείνου μὲν εὐτυχεῖς μέρος.
Εκ. ὦ φίλταθ', ὡς εὖ κἀξίως λέγεις σέθεν. 990

Πλ. τί δῆτα βούλῃ δεύτερον μαθεῖν ἐμοῦ ;

Εκ. εἰ τῆς τεκούσης τῆσδε . . . μέμνηταί τί μου ;

Πλ. καὶ δεῦρό γ' ὡς σὲ κρύφιος ἐζήτει μολεῖν.

Εκ. [after a pause] χρυσὸς δὲ σῶς ὃν ἦλθεν ἐκ Τροίας ἔχων ;

Πλ. σῶς, ἐν δόμοις γε τοῖς ἐμοῖς φρουρούμενος.   995

Εκ. σῶσόν νυν αὐτὸν μηδ' ἔρα τῶν πλησίον.

Πλ. ἥκιστ'· ὀναίμην τοῦ παρόντος, ὦ γύναι.

Hecuba. Ah, so you know my news for you and your
          sons ?

Polymestor. I do not know it.   You have yet to tell me.

Hecuba. There is, O friend, beloved as now I love
          you . . .   1000

Polymestor. What would you have me and my children
          know ?

Hecuba. A buried treasury of the house of Priam . . .

Polymestor. Of which you wish your son to hear the
          secret . . .

Hecuba. Yes, yes.   From you, my true, religious friend.

Polymestor. Why fetch my children then ?   What need ot
          them ?   1005

Hecuba. In case you die . . . better for them to know.

Polymestor. That is well thought of.   Yes, it is wiser so.

Hecuba. Come then, you know Athene's shrine in Troy ?

Polymestor. Is the gold there ?   What clue is left to guide
          me ?

Hecuba. A black stone jutting from the level ground.   1010

Polymestor [*after a pause*].   Has Troy some other secret
          you would tell me ?

Hecuba. I have brought some treasures . . . I would have
          you guard them.

Polymestor. Here . . . on your person ?   Have you hidden
          them ?

Hecuba. Yes, safe, here, in the house, in a heap of the
          spoil.

Polymestor. What, here, in the camp ?   In the barracks of
          the Greeks ?   1015

Hecuba. The women prisoners lodge by themselves.

Polymestor. Are there no men here ?   Is all safe in the
          house ?

Hecuba. There 's no Greek here.   We women are alone.
　　Come in, come in.   The Greeks impatiently
　　Await the hoisting of the sails for home.　　　1020
　　We'll do your business . . . then, go back, and take
　　Your children with you . . . where you have lodged my
　　　son.

[POLYMESTOR *and the children, followed by* HECUBA, *enter
　　the house.   The door is closed.*]

Chorus.

Thou hast not paid, but soon shalt pay, the price.
　　His voyage of gain is over.
　　His good ship reels : he falls　　　　　　　　1025
　　Lost in a hungry sea :
　　And the price that he pays is Life.
　　When the Gods and Justice meet,
　　And the Pledge that is forfeited,
　　The end is Ruin.　　　　　　　　　　　　1030
Thy hope shall prove a cheat : thou art beguiled
　　To death, ah wretched !
　　And thou shalt not die by the sword.

[*After a moment's silence, cries are heard within.*]

Πλ. [*within*]
　　　　ὤμοι, τυφλοῦμαι φέγγος ὀμμάτων τάλας.　1035
Χο. —　ἠκούσατ᾽ ἀνδρὸς Θρῃκὸς οἰμωγήν, φίλαι ;
Πλ.　　ὤμοι μάλ᾽ αὖθις, τέκνα, δυστήνου σφαγῆς.
Χο. —　φίλαι, πέπρακται καίν᾽ ἔσω δόμων κακά.
Πλ.　　ἀλλ᾽ οὔτι μὴ φύγητε λαιψηρῷ ποδί·
　　　　βάλλων γὰρ οἴκων τῶνδ᾽ ἀναρρήξω μυχούς.　1040
Χο. —　ἰδού, βαρείας χειρὸς ὁρμᾶται βέλος.
　　—　βούλεσθ᾽ ἐπεσπέσωμεν ; ὡς ἀκμὴ καλεῖ
　　　　Ἑκάβῃ παρεῖναι Τρῳάσιν τε συμμάχους.
Εκ. [*within*]. ἄρασσε, φείδου μηδέν, ἐκβάλλων πύλας·
　　　　οὐ γάρ ποτ᾽ ὄμμα λαμπρὸν ἐνθήσεις κόραις,　1045
　　　　οὐ παῖδας ὄψῃ ζῶντας οὓς ἔκτειν᾽ ἐγώ.

[HECUBA *opens the doors and comes out. The noise of*
POLYMESTOR *battering at the walls, which he has mistaken
for the doors, continues.*]

Χο. ἢ γὰρ καθεῖλες Θρῆκα, καὶ κρατεῖς, ξένον,
   δέσποινα, καὶ δέδρακας οἷάπερ λέγεις ;

Εκ. ὄψῃ νιν αὐτίκ᾽ ὄντα δωμάτων πάρος
   τυφλὸν τυφλῷ στείχοντα παραφόρῳ ποδί,   1050
   παίδων τε δισσῶν σώμαθ᾽, οὓς ἔκτειν᾽ ἐγὼ
   σὺν ταῖς ἀρίσταις Τρῳάσιν· δίκην δέ μοι
   δέδωκε. χωρεῖ δ᾽, ὡς ὁρᾷς, ὅδ᾽ ἐκ δόμων.
   ἀλλ᾽ ἐκποδὼν ἄπειμι κἀποστήσομαι
   θυμῷ ζέοντι Θρῃκὶ δυσμαχωτάτῳ.   1055

[*She goes down among the Chorus. The Thracian is heard
at first within, still trying to catch the women.*]

Πλ.   ὤμοι ἐγώ, πᾷ βῶ,
      πᾷ στῶ, πᾷ κέλσω ;
      τετράποδος βάσιν θηρὸς ὀρεστέρου
      τιθέμενος ἐπίχειρα κατ᾽ ἴχνος ; ποίαν
      ἢ ταύταν ἢ τάνδ᾽ ἐξαλλάξω, τὰς   1060
      ἀνδροφόνους μάρψαι χρῄζων Ἰλιάδας,
      αἵ με διώλεσαν ;
      τάλαιναι κόραι τάλαιναι Φρυγῶν,
         ὦ κατάρατοι,   1065
      ποῖ καί με φυγᾷ πτώσσουσι μυχῶν ;

[*He appears during the last speech in the doorway, and
gropes his way forward. Though he is blind he can feel
the warmth of the sun.*]

      εἴθε μοι ὀμμάτων αἱματόεν βλέφαρον
      ἀκέσαι᾽ ἀκέσαιο τυφλόν, Ἅλιε,
      φέγγος ἐπαλλάξας.

         Ah, Ah,
   Silence . . . I hear footsteps . . . the stealthy steps of
      the women !   1070

Let me leap on them, and glut myself
  On their flesh and their bones,
And make my feast on these savage creatures,
And torture them, for the price of my shame and tor-
  ment.
         Ah, misery.   1075
  Where am I going? Alas!
I have left my children alone for these Bacchants of
  Death to tear
And mangle and leave on the wild mountain-side
  For the ravening dogs to eat.
  Which way? Where can I rest?   1080
I will wrap my robe about me,
As a ship that makes for harbour, and shortens sail, I
  will go
  Back, to watch over my children,
  Into the wild beast's lair.

Chorus. Wretched! A terrible thing is wrought on
    thee.   1085
  Thy deeds were shameful. Dreadful are the wages
  Allotted by the hand of Destiny.

Polymestor. Aiai!
  To arms, my spearmen, soldiers, Knights of the
    Thracian breed.   1090
    To arms!
  Ho Greeks! Ho Princes! Rescue, rescue, help!
    Quick, quick! In God's name, help!

Do they hear? No help? Oh, why are you so slow?
The women have destroyed me, the captive women.

      Horrible, horrible!   1095
    Alas, shame, torment!
Where can I turn? What place is there for me?
If I fly to the height, to the hall of heaven,   1100
  Is not Orion there, and Sirius,
With eyes that are flames of fire?
  Or, wretched, shall I plunge into the flood of
    darkness
  That leads to the home of Death?

Chorus. If man's calamity passeth endurance
  He may take leave of life, and none shall blame him.

[*Enter* AGAMEMNON, *attended.*]

Αγ. κραυγῆς ἀκούσας ἦλθον· οὐ γὰρ ἥσυχος
πέτρας ὀρείας παῖς λέλακ' ἀνὰ στρατὸν   1110
Ἠχὼ διδοῦσα θόρυβον· εἰ δὲ μὴ Φρυγῶν
πύργους πεσόντας ᾖσμεν Ἑλλήνων δορί,
φόβον παρέσχεν οὐ μέσως ὅδε κτύπος.

Πλ. ὦ φίλτατ'· ᾐσθόμην γάρ, Ἀγάμεμνον, σέθεν
φωνῆς ἀκούσας· εἰσορᾷς ἃ πάσχομεν;   1115

Αγ. ἔα·
Πολυμῆστορ· ὦ δύστηνε, τίς σ' ἀπώλεσεν;
τίς ὄμμ' ἔθηκε τυφλὸν αἱμάξας κόρας,
παῖδάς τε τούσδ' ἔκτεινεν; ἦ μέγαν χόλον
σοὶ καὶ τέκνοισιν εἶχεν ὅστις ἦν ἄρα.

Πλ. Ἑκάβη με σὺν γυναιξὶν αἰχμαλωτίσιν   1120
ἀπώλεσ'—οὐκ ἀπώλεσ', ἀλλὰ μειζόνως.

Αγ. τί φής; σὺ τοὔργον εἴργασαι τόδ', ὡς λέγει;
σὺ τόλμαν, Ἑκάβη, τήνδ' ἔτλης ἀμήχανον;

Πλ. ὤμοι, τί λέξεις; ἦ γὰρ ἐγγύς ἐστί που;
σήμηνον, εἰπὲ ποῦ 'σθ', ἵν' ἁρπάσας χεροῖν   1125
διασπάσωμαι καὶ καθαιμάξω χρόα.

[*He rushes forward, but is seized by* AGAMEMNON'S *Guards.*]

Αγ. οὗτος, τί πάσχεις;   Πλ. πρὸς θεῶν σε λίσσομαι,
μέθες μ' ἐφεῖναι τῇδε μαργῶσαν χέρα.

Αγ. ἴσχ'· ἐκβαλὼν δὲ καρδίας τὸ βάρβαρον
λέγ', ὡς ἀκούσας σοῦ τε τῆσδέ τ' ἐν μέρει   1130
κρίνω δικαίως ἀνθ' ὅτου πάσχεις τάδε.

Πλ. λέγοιμ' ἄν. ἦν τις Πριαμιδῶν νεώτατος,
Πολύδωρος, Ἑκάβης παῖς, ὃν ἐκ Τροίας ἐμοὶ
πατὴρ δίδωσι Πρίαμος ἐν δόμοις τρέφειν,
ὕποπτος ὢν δὴ Τρωικῆς ἁλώσεως.
τοῦτον κατέκτειν'· ἀνθ' ὅτου δ' ἔκτεινά νιν,   1135
ἄκουσον, ὡς εὖ καὶ σοφῇ προμηθίᾳ.
ἔδεισα μὴ σοὶ πολέμιος λειφθεὶς ὁ παῖς
Τροίαν ἀθροίσῃ καὶ ξυνοικίσῃ πάλιν,

γνόντες δ' Ἀχαιοὶ ζῶντα Πριαμιδῶν τινα   1140
Φρυγῶν ἐς αἶαν αὖθις ἄρειαν στόλον,
κἄπειτα Θρῄκης πεδία τρίβοιεν τάδε
λεηλατοῦντες, γείτοσιν δ' εἴη κακὸν
Τρώων, ἐν ᾧπερ νῦν, ἄναξ, ἐκάμνομεν.

Hecuba, learning how her son had perished,   1145
Contrived a lie to bring me here, a tale
Of Priam's golden treasure hid in Troy,
To which she would direct me.   Privily,
That none might know the secret, to the house
She took me, with my children.   On a couch   1150
I sat, and clustered round me, right and left,
Were many Trojan women, with pretence
Of friendly entertainment, pressing close
To see my robes, and flattering the skill
Of Thracian needles.   Some, as curious
To view my foreign weapons, took away   1155
My spears, and so disarmed me.   Matrons nursed
My children, and made much of them, and still
Passed them from hand to hand, away from me.
Then, Oh incredible, mid that friendly murmur,   1160
With a sudden stir, a glint of steel from their robes,
They stabbed my children, and, like cuttle-fishes,
Caught me, and twined about my legs and arms,
And held me fast, longing to help my children,
And yet I could not.   If I raised my head,   1165
They held me back by the hair.   I could not move
A hand ; they swarmed on me ; I could do nothing,
Nothing, alas !   And last, and worst of all,
They did this deed of horror, seized the pins
That held their raiment, plunged them in these
    eyes,   1170
And blinded me with gore, then, scattering,
Fled from my vengeance.   Like a beast at bay,
I leapt on them, hunting the hounds of blood,
And beat the trail of them along the walls
With blows and battering.   This, Agamemnon,
This I have suffered, in my zeal for you,   1175
Because I killed your enemy.   What need
For talk ?   The sum of all the infamies

The tongues of men, past, present, and to come,
Ascribe to woman, I'll endorse, and say   1180
There's no such monster bred on land or sea;
And none has dealings with their kind, but knows it.

Chorus. Control your passion. Seek not to condemn
All womankind in one because you suffer.

Hecuba. Agamemnon, never ought the tongues of
men   1186
To plead more eloquently than the truth.
Good men should prove good speakers, and the bad,
Their very argument grown rank, should find   1190
No specious words to colour evil deeds.
Oh, they are strict professors of the art,
And they are wise; yet in the end of all,
Not wise enough. They perish. None escapes.
Let this, my lord, serve for my opening   1195
To you: and now for him! I'll argue too!
    You say, to spare the Greeks another war,
For Agamemnon's sake, you killed my son.
So, firstly, scoundrel, never can the Greeks   1200
Be friends with us barbarians. Oh no,
They cannot! And what hope had you of favour
To make you zealous? Marriage with a Greek?
Were you their kinsman? Had you any pretext?
The Greeks might come again, the Greeks might come
And ravage Thrace! Who, think you, will believe
    it?   1205
No, it was gold, if you would tell the truth,
Your lust for gold murdered this son of mine.

ἐπεὶ δίδαξον τοῦτο· πῶς, ὅτ᾽ εὐτύχει
Τροία, πέριξ δὲ πύργος εἶχ᾽ ἔτι πτόλιν,
ἔζη τε Πρίαμος Ἕκτορός τ᾽ ἤνθει δόρυ,   1210
τί δ᾽ οὐ τότ᾽, εἴπερ τῷδ᾽ ἐβουλήθης χάριν
θέσθαι, τρέφων τὸν παῖδα κἂν δόμοις ἔχων
ἔκτεινας ἢ ζῶντ᾽ ἦλθες Ἀργείοις ἄγων;
ἀλλ᾽ ἡνίχ᾽ ἡμεῖς οὐκέτ᾽ ἐσμὲν ἐν φάει—
καπνῷ δ᾽ ἐσήμην᾽ ἄστυ—πολεμίων ὕπο,   1215
ξένον κατέκτας σὴν μολόντ᾽ ἐφ᾽ ἑστίαν.
    πρὸς τοῖσδε νῦν ἄκουσον, ὡς φανῇς κακός.

χρῆν σ᾽, εἴπερ ἦσθα τοῖς Ἀχαιοῖσιν φίλος,
τὸν χρυσὸν ὃν φῂς οὐ σὸν ἀλλὰ τοῦδ᾽ ἔχειν
δοῦναι φέροντα πενομένοις τε καὶ χρόνον   1220
πολὺν πατρῴας γῆς ἀπεξενωμένοις·
σὺ δ᾽ οὐδὲ νῦν πω σῆς ἀπαλλάξαι χερὸς
τολμᾷς, ἔχων δὲ καρτερεῖς ἔτ᾽ ἐν δόμοις.
καὶ μὴν τρέφων μὲν ὥς σε παῖδ᾽ ἐχρῆν τρέφειν
σώσας τε τὸν ἐμόν, εἶχες ἂν καλὸν κλέος·   1225
ἐν τοῖς κακοῖς γὰρ ἀγαθοὶ σαφέστατοι
φίλοι· τὰ χρηστὰ δ᾽ αὔθ᾽ ἕκαστ᾽ ἔχει φίλους.
εἰ δ᾽ ἐσπάνιζες χρημάτων, ὃ δ᾽ εὐτύχει,
θησαυρὸς ἄν σοι παῖς ὑπῆρχ᾽ οὑμὸς μέγας·
νῦν δ᾽ οὔτ᾽ ἐκεῖνον ἄνδρ᾽ ἔχεις σαυτῷ φίλον,   1230
χρυσοῦ τ᾽ ὄνησις οἴχεται παῖδές τε σοί,
αὐτός τε πράσσεις ὧδε.   σοὶ δ᾽ ἐγὼ λέγω,
Ἀγάμεμνον, εἰ τῷδ᾽ ἀρκέσεις, κακὸς φανῇ·
οὔτ᾽ εὐσεβῆ γὰρ οὔτε πιστὸν οἷς ἐχρῆν,
οὐχ ὅσιον, οὐ δίκαιον εὖ δράσεις ξένον·   1235
αὐτὸν δὲ χαίρειν τοῖς κακοῖς σὲ φήσομεν
τοιοῦτον ὄντα . . . δεσπότας δ᾽ οὐ λοιδορῶ.

Χα. φεῦ φεῦ· βροτοῖσιν ὡς τὰ χρηστὰ πράγματα
χρηστῶν ἀφορμὰς ἐνδίδωσ᾽ ἀεὶ λόγων.

Αγ. ἀχθεινὰ μέν μοι τἀλλότρια κρίνειν κακά,   1240
ὅμως δ᾽ ἀνάγκη· καὶ γὰρ αἰσχύνην φέρει,
πρᾶγμ᾽ ἐς χέρας λαβόντ᾽ ἀπώσασθαι τόδε.
ἐμοὶ δ᾽, ἵν᾽ εἰδῇς, οὔτ᾽ ἐμὴν δοκεῖς χάριν
οὔτ᾽ οὖν Ἀχαιῶν ἄνδρ᾽ ἀποκτεῖναι ξένον,
ἀλλ᾽ ὡς ἔχῃς τὸν χρυσὸν ἐν δόμοισι σοῖς.   1245
λέγεις δὲ σαυτῷ πρόσφορ᾽ ἐν κακοῖσιν ὤν.
τάχ᾽ οὖν παρ᾽ ὑμῖν ῥᾴδιον ξενοκτονεῖν·
ἡμῖν δέ γ᾽ αἰσχρὸν τοῖσιν Ἕλλησιν τόδε.
πῶς οὖν σε κρίνας μὴ ἀδικεῖν φύγω ψόγον;
οὐκ ἂν δυναίμην.   ἀλλ᾽ ἐπεὶ τὰ μὴ καλὰ   1250
πράσσειν ἐτόλμας, τλῆθι καὶ τὰ μὴ φίλα.

Polymestor. Oh ignominy! Beaten by a woman,
　　Sentenced by thralls, defeated by a slave!
Hecuba. Is not the sentence just? Did you not wrong me?
Polymestor. Alas! My children! Oh, I am blind and
　　childless.　　　　　　　　　　　　　　　1255
Hecuba. It hurts? What of my son? Have I not
　　suffered?
Polymestor. O devilish joy, to triumph in such outrage.
Hecuba. O righteous joy, to triumph in just vengeance.
Polymestor. A joy soon ended, when the watery waste—
Hecuba. The sea, that waits to carry me to Greece—
Polymestor. Waits—to engulf you—flung from the ship's
　　top-gallant—　　　　　　　　　　　　1261
Hecuba. What strange adventure? Who shall force me
　　to it?
Polymestor. Yourself—mounting the mast, of your own
　　motion,
Hecuba. Can such things be? Shall I find wings, and fly?
Polymestor. In the body of a dog, with eyes of fire.　1265
Hecuba. So? Must I be so changed? How can you
　　know it?
Polymestor. The Thracian prophet-god, Dionysus, told
　　me.
Hecuba. And told you nothing of your own disasters?
Polymestor. No, all your cunning had not trapped me
　　then.
Hecuba [*after a pause*]. Must I live on, to haunt this place,
　　or die?　　　　　　　　　　　　　　　1270
Polymestor. Die must you, but your grave shall bear this
　　name—
Hecuba. A name to tell the story of my change?
Polymestor. This name, a mariner's sign, the Hell-Hound's
　　Tomb.
Hecuba. I am revenged, revenged, and I care nothing.

[*There is silence for a moment.*]

Polymestor. Cassandra is your child. She must die too.
Hecuba. On your own head—thus, thus, I spit your curse!
Polymestor. Agamemnon's wife, the wife of hate, shall kill
　　her.　　　　　　　　　　　　　　　　1277
Hecuba [*breaking down*]. God keep the Tyndarid woman
　　from such madness.

[HECUBA *sinks to the ground, and is silent for the rest of the scene.*]

Polymestor. You, Agamemnon, too.   Her axe awaits you.

Agamemnon. You court destruction, fellow. Are you mad ?

Polymestor. Kill me.   A bath of blood waits you . . . in
    Argos.   1281

Agamemnon. Seize him. Convey him hence. Away with
    him !

Polymestor. You hear me, and it hurts you ? *Agamemnon.*
    Stop his mouth.

Polymestor. Aye, stop my mouth, for all is said. *Agamem-
    non.* Away !

    He brags too boldly.   Let him be confined   1285
    In savage solitude on some desolate island.
    Go, miserable Hecuba, and bury
    Your children.   Trojan women, it is time
    To seek your masters' quarters, for I find
    The wind blows fairly for the homeward voyage.   1290
    So be the journey fair, and all at home
    Prove kind, and all these troubles end in good.

[*The Chorus chant, as they pass out of the orchestra.*]

Chorus. Come away, dear ones, come away.
    To the camp, to the place of the ships, to the sea,
    To the strange new life of slavery,
    For all are the slaves of Destiny.   1295

NOTES

This famous ghost is the ancestor, through Seneca, of many Elizabethan ghosts, notably Hamlet's father and the victims of King Richard III. But this is not the first ghost-scene in tragedy. In the *Persae*, Darius is raised by oriental incantations: in the *Eumenides*, Clytaemnestra's spirit wakes the Furies: in the *Polyxena* of Sophocles, the shade of Achilles came from the tomb with the words—which Euripides remembers here—

> From the dark deep of Acheron's lifeless flood,
> The coast that knows no music save the noise
> Of cries and beating of the breast, I come.

There are some fine lines also quoted from a Latin tragedy—perhaps the *Ilione* of Pacuvius, which told the Polydorus story—

> Adsum atque advenio Acherunte vix via alta atque ardua
> Per speluncas saxis structas asperis pendentibus
> Maximis, ubi rigida constat caeca caligo inferum.

Senecan and Elizabethan ghosts clamour for vengeance. The spirit of Polydorus asks for no such thing: simply, he cannot rest in Hades till he is buried. So in Homer, the ghost of Patroclus does not ask his friend for vengeance (Achilles is insulting Hector's body, and planning to sacrifice Trojan prisoners), but complains of the delay in burial: 'You sleep, Achilles, and are grown forgetful. ... Bury me quickly. ... The souls of the dead keep me far off, and do not allow me to join their company and pass the river. I wander vainly up and down the broad-gated House of Hades'. (Elsewhere Homer talks of the House of Hades 'in the hiding-places of the earth', as a 'grim and ghastly mansion which even the gods hate'.) Polymestor's victim craves not the vengeance which Hecuba so tragically gives her, but only peace in the grave.

3. Euripides makes Hecuba the daughter of a Thracian prince, whose name is derived from the sacred ivy (κισσός) of the savage Thracian Dionysus. The god himself was sometimes called Κισσεύς. Hecuba, like her enemy, has a touch of Thracian savagery, and she becomes 'a Bacchant of Death' (1077). In Homer's story she is a Phrygian, daughter of Dymas.

8. The Thracian Chersonese is the modern peninsula of Gallipoli, which is thus described by Mr. Masefield: 'Those who wish to imagine the scene must think of twenty miles of any rough and steep sea-coast known to them, picturing it as roadless, much broken with gullies, covered with scrub, sandy, loose, and difficult

to walk on, and never more than two miles of accessible landing throughout its length'. The shape and colouring of the hills is beautiful, and sometimes reminded Mr. Masefield of the northern coast of Cornwall.

13. ὅ adverbial accusative = δι' ὅ in meaning. Translate 'and that is why . . .'

14. ὅπλα, 'armour', especially the hoplite's heavy shield. In Homer Polydorus is the youngest, dearest son of Priam, by Laothoe, not Hecuba. Priam forbids him to fight ; he disobeys, and is killed by Achilles.

16. 'So long as the boundary-stones of the country remained up-right', i. e. until the Greeks overthrew them, as the sign of the completion of their conquest. Both private lands and state territories normally had boundary stones, which showed the limits of the property, and were suitably inscribed, to show who was the rightful owner. So, when the Athenian king Theseus conquered the Megarid, he put up a pillar on the boundary inscribed on the near side, 'This is Ionia, not Peloponnese', and on the far side, 'This is Peloponnese, not Ionia'. When the Spartans reconquered the country, they destroyed the stone. Similarly the Greek conquerors have not only burnt Troy but systematically overthrown the boundary-stones throughout the Troad, to show that the land no longer belongs to its former owners.

22. The hearth in every Greek home was sacred, and the destruction of the royal hearth symbolizes the complete ruin of the State.

23. Neoptolemus murdered Priam though he had taken refuge at the altar of Zeus. The reference to this gross act of impiety is meant to prepare us for the part played by Neoptolemus in the sacrifice of Polyxena.

28. 'Sometimes on the shore, sometimes . . .' The omission of the first ἄλλοτε is idiomatic. (So Sophocles has ταῦρος, ἄλλοτ' αἰόλος δράκων of Deianeira's monstrous suitor ; 'he came sometimes as a bull, sometimes as a snake'.)

29. διαύλοις carried backwards and forwards by the waves, like a chariot racing up and down the double course.

30. From the ghost of Patroclus onwards, visions and dreams in Greek literature hover *over the head* of the person who sees them, so that the words ὑπὲρ μητρὸς φίλης . . . ἀίσσω mean, as the scholiast says, 'I appear to her in a dream'. Hecuba herself says she has had 'dreams', one of her son, the other about her daughter. She only has time to tell of the latter, when she is interrupted by the Chorus. But the audience knows all about the former, since the prologue *is*, in effect, the dream.

ἄκλαυτος ἄταφος. So Achilles says 'The body of my friend Patroclus is lying by the ships, unwept, unburied'.

32. 'And this is the third day'. τριταῖον practically = τρίτον, and ὅσονπερ means 'through all the time in which . . .'

At line 55 the central doors of the skene begin to open, and at 59 the voice of Hecuba is heard within. Supported by her women, she comes forward, until at line 68 she is in the open sunlight. Her purpose in coming is to publish to the air and light the terrifying dreams which have been haunting her. The Greeks believed that bad dreams might be made harmless (*a*) if the dreamer told them aloud in the sunlight, and (*b*) if he prayed, or performed a propitiatory ceremony to the gods. The technical formula for such a ceremony is used by Hecuba at line 73 in connexion with her solemn appeal to the light of day, the night, and earth (i. e. to the powers above and the powers below). She relates the dream about Polyxena, which she connects with the appearance of Achilles to the Greeks, and then repeats the formula ('I cry it aloud to avert it' 73, and 'Give ear ... and avert it' 96). Before she has time to perform the same ceremony for the dream about Polydorus, the Chorus brings news that Polyxena has been chosen for sacrifice.

68. The *Hecuba* of Ennius contained a similar appeal to the powers of day and night, 'O magna templa caelitum commixta stellis splendidis'.

79. She invokes the nether gods because dreams come from the earth; but there is tragic irony; she is really, though she does not know it, praying for the dead.

80. Ships carried several anchors, and the 'last anchor' became proverbial for a last hope.

87. 'The divinely inspired prophet Helenus' (cf. βίη Ἡρακλῆος 'mighty Heracles') was not dead, but worse, a traitor. Before the capture of Troy, he had been taken by Odysseus, and had prophesied for the Greeks, revealing to them the means by which Troy could be taken. Sophocles tells the story in the *Philoctetes*, and the painter Polygnotus, in his picture of the Sack of Troy, which Euripides must have seen at Delphi, introduced Helenus 'clad in a purple mantle and seated in an attitude of dejection', full of remorse for what he had done. His later life, as a dependant of Neoptolemus and the inheritor of his kingdom in Epirus, is told by Virgil, *Aen*. iii. Andromache, who was assigned to Neoptolemus as his prize, was deserted by him for Hermione, and given as wife to Helenus. Virgil represents her as still faithful to the memory of Hector, and protesting that the fate of Polyxena is preferable to her own. In the same famous picture Polygnotus represented Polyxena 'with her hair braided as a virgin', and Neoptolemus as still savagely killing Trojans after the fighting was done.

88. This is the first mention of Cassandra, whose fate is contrasted throughout the play with that of Polyxena. The prophetess, sacred to Apollo, had now become the slave of Agamemnon, with whom, as every one knows, she was murdered by his wife Clytaemnestra when he brought her home to Argos.

108. λέγεται δόξαι, 'the resolution is said to have been carried', lit. 'it is said to have seemed good . . .' The phrase recalls the language of the Athenian Assembly (e. g. ἔδοξε τῷ δήμῳ). So far as

outward formality is concerned, the decision is lawful. But it violates the laws of heaven, though it is passed from motives of superstitious loyalty to Achilles.

110. We should say 'You know how', where Greek says 'You know when . . .'

111. σχεδίας, 'transports': the word often means 'rafts', and suggests the crowded decks of the flat-bottomed transport-ships.

112. 'Though they had their sails already straining against the ropes', i.e. already secured by the fore-stays to the mast-head, and ready for the voyage.

122. The prophetess is Cassandra. Agamemnon, as king, ought not to have allowed his passion for the captive to influence his judgement. He was right in opposing the human sacrifice, but his motive was wrong.

This touch reveals his character. He is the typical weak king who puts private before public considerations. So later on, he ought to give Hecuba justice and bring Polymestor to trial on public grounds. He shirks the responsibility, because he is afraid of unpopularity. But he consents to shut his eyes to anything Hecuba does, because she is Cassandra's mother.

123. Theseus was the heroic king to whom the Athenians looked back as the founder of their greatness. His two sons, true Athenians, took different views and argued for them, but agreed that public interests must go before private, and so demanded the sacrifice. Euripides represents the Greeks as genuinely convinced. He does not, of course, approve, nor would any of the audience. But although human sacrifice is for the Athenian democracy a wickedness of the past, the argument 'we ought to be harsh . . . in honour of the memory of our dead' was often heard in Athens during the Peloponnesian war. Odysseus is regarded by the captive women as a scoundrel. When he appears, we shall see, he is simply a typical 'statesman', taking a 'practical' view, unsympathetic, not necessarily insincere.

160. This scene is parodied in Aristophanes' *Clouds*. Old Strepsiades, trying to learn cunning from Socrates, has to wrap up in a blanket and lie still thinking, but unfortunately the blanket is not very clean:—

Streps. Alas! Oh! Ow! Alas! *Chorus.* What ails thee? What is thy sorrow? *Streps.* O wretched, I am lost. Out of the bedding come the Corinthians [a pun on κόρεις, bugs]: they come, they bite, they tear my ribs, they drink my life. . . . *Chor.* Be not so passionate in grief! *Streps.* How can I bear it? My money gone, complexion gone, my life-blood gone, and slippers gone . . . and there is not much left of ME!'

169. Hecuba was at first supported by other women, and hardly able to stand. The bad news has nerved her to an effort. She refuses help, and insists on going to the hut by herself. In English it seems comic to address one's own legs, but the effect is not comic in Greek. Translate 'wretched limbs', and all is well.

171. ὦ τέκνον, ὦ παῖ. This pathetic repetition seems to have struck Aristophanes as comic. Anyhow he uses the phrase with comic effect in the *Clouds*. When Strepsiades comes to fetch home his son from the 'Thinking-Shop', the excited old man cries 'Come forth, my son, my child, come forth and listen to thy father's voice'. Socrates produces him with the tragic words 'Behold the man', and Strepsiades breaks out again 'Oh, oh, my love, my dear, oh, oh, hurray, hurray, hurray!'

197. Polyxena is frightened before she hears the news. When she first hears it, she does not grasp it completely, and wants it repeated. But when once she realizes, she thinks only of her mother's unhappiness, not at all of her own misfortune. It is important to remember that Polyxena is standing silent, listening, while Odysseus talks with Hecuba in the next scene.

218. From the first moment Euripides makes us realize how clever Odysseus is. The Chorus pretend—for his benefit—that they do not know what he has come about. In his first words he quietly makes it clear that he has noticed.

γύναι, 'Madam'. His tone is formal, but scrupulously polite.

222. ἡμᾶς. Odysseus is attended by armed guards.

224. Neoptolemus is naturally chosen for this office.

223-4. As ἐπιστάτης N. will arrange the ritual, and as ἱερεύς he will himself kill the victim.

225. οἶσθ' οὖν ὃ δράσον; In the fairly common phrase, the imperative is equivalent to 'you must do'. ἀποσπασθῇς, lit. 'do not be dragged away . . .', i. e. 'do not force us to drag you away'.

227. Recognize what your strength is (i. e. how weak you are) and how bad is your situation (what evils are present to you).

228. ἃ δεῖ φρονεῖν, 'to have the thoughts which one ought to have', is a regular phrase for 'to be rightminded' and 'to be sensible'. Odysseus uses the proverbial morality which bids men 'know themselves', be quiet and modest, and not struggle against overwhelming odds.

229. A well-known critic has objected to these lines as too rhetorical. He says that 'Full of lament, not destitute of tears' is intolerable. Perhaps the translation

> Alas! So it has come, a tragedy
> Of clamorous grief—yes, and some tears to shed,

may serve to show that the effect of the Greek is not really so bad.

ἀγών means 'a struggle', but—as the English word 'agony' reminds us—can apply to a spiritual as well as a physical struggle.

231. We should say 'when'. The Greek idiom can say 'where', in the sense of 'in the situation in which . . .'

232. τρέφει, keeps me alive.

233. κακῶν, the genitive is governed by the comparative μείζονα.

236. μὲν . . . δέ. English does not balance its clauses in just this way. Translate 'just as it was your lawful right to speak, so it is right that we, who question you, should have an answer'.

239. οἶσθ' ἡνίκα is like οἶσθ' ὅτε 110.

249. ἐμός emphatic: 'you were my slave then, as I am yours now'.

250. This touch is true to life. Odysseus, suddenly reminded of this crisis in his past, does not exactly remember what he promised. So he cynically exclaims that, whatever it may have been, he is not bound by 'mere words', designed to serve the occasion. When he has had time to reflect, he takes a different line. He persuades himself that his promise only was to protect Hecuba himself, so that, in conscience, he is not bound to save her child.

254 ff. These lines are said almost 'aside'. By her phrase 'May I not even know you', Hecuba ingeniously turns the point of her own attack, making it possible to interpret her words as not applying to Odysseus.

265. The reference to Helen is dramatically important, as leading up naturally to the curse on Helen at the end of the scene. That, in its turn, leads up to the cursing of Helen by the Chorus (943 ff.).

286. Just as Odysseus has bidden Hecuba show the self-restraint, the prudence which is proverbially appropriate in misfortune, so Hecuba bids him show the moderation which befits the strong, and the αἰδώς (reverence) which is due from the strong to the weak. She has shown that neither necessity nor justice demand this sacrifice. Her last and strongest argument remains, that the sacrifice is a violation of the Greeks' own law, likely to arouse the indignation (φθόνος) of gods and men. The Trojan women took refuge at the altars, and were taken by the Greeks from their place of sanctuary. According to Greek ideas, their lives having been thus spared, they were now under the protection of the Greeks, who were bound by all the laws of religion to spare them.

291 ff. Athens particularly prided herself—and sometimes, in moments of irritation blamed herself—for treating slaves as human beings.

293. λέγῃ second person singular: 'though they may abuse you' for pleading an unpopular cause, your authority will carry the day.

300. φρενός depends on τῷ θυμουμένῳ, which practically means 'passion'.

306-7. ἐν τῷδε ... ὅταν is not quite logical, but natural enough: 'In this respect ... when'. Strict logic would demand 'that ...'

317 ff. There is no reason to regard this insistence on the gratitude due to the dead, and on the desire for glory in the grave, as insincere. When Odysseus suddenly turns on Hecuba with the suggestion that perhaps, as a barbarian, she cannot understand such loyalty to the dead, a Greek audience could not help sympathizing with him. The sequel makes all this highly dramatic, for Hecuba herself, in mistaken loyalty to her own dead,

exacts an appalling vengeance from Polymestor, killing his innocent children, as well as blinding the criminal . . . and loses her own humanity in the act. The whole play must have been felt as a damaging attack on 'statesmen' who justify acts of barbarism and cruelty on the plea that 'the dead must not have died in vain'.

342. Odysseus hides his hand in his robe and turns his head away because he is afraid that Polyxena will touch his hand or beard in supplication: if she can do this, she will be in some degree sacred, and he will feel bound to treat her as a suppliant.

352. ζῆλον ἔχουσα does not mean 'being zealous' but rather 'having zeal shown about me'. The word γάμων explains the object of the zeal, and this is further explained by the indirect question ὅτου, &c. 'And there was much rivalry for marriage with me, much contention, to whose hearth and home I should come.'

359. The shift from plural to singular, and from optative to future indicative makes the possibility more vivid. English can give the same effect: 'I might fall into the hands of cruel masters, one who will'.

363. Work at the loom, the tasks of bread-making (grinding the corn and baking), cleaning the house, and making the household garments, are the normal work of captive serving-women, in Homer's time as later. But for Polyxena the worst humiliation is not this household drudgery, but the prospect of being forced into marriage with a slave. By death Polyxena preserves her modesty and chastity. The idea recurs at the moment of her death. Polyxena's happiness, in spite of all misfortunes, is thus contrasted with the shameful fate of Cassandra. When Hecuba brings herself to plead with Agamemnon on the ground that Cassandra is his slave, her humiliation is the more tragic because she is Polyxena's mother.

367. Prose might say 'While I am free, I give up the light'. ἐλεύθερον is poetically made to agree with φέγγος, and the sense is 'I give up the light while it is still the light of freedom'.

370. Notice that του has no accent, and is therefore not the definite article.

371. παρ' ἡμῖν, 'with us' (i.e. in our situation). θάρσος is 'a ground for confidence', and the genitives ἐλπίδος and δόξης mean 'consisting of hope or thought': χρή practically means 'it is my destiny'.

372. Greek says 'Mother, and you . . .', where we say 'And you, mother, . . .' Translate in the English way. μηδέν, adverbial.

373. Supply μήτε before λέγουσα (cf. 28). μοι is governed by συν in the compound verb, which governs θανεῖν as its object. Take μὴ κατ' ἀξίαν together.

376. Supply ζυγόν as object to φέρει.

377. 'Would be happier rather by dying than . . .' Polyxena begs her mother to wish, like herself, for death rather than dishonour. In the sequel Hecuba sacrifices every scruple to her lust for vengeance. By making Polyxena care so much about her mother's honour, Euripides prepares us to feel the thrill of that humiliation.

379. The Greek word χαρακτήρ, used here, is the origin of our 'character'. It means the stamp, or impression, made by the die on a coin (cf. Milton's phrase 'Reason's mintage | Charáctered in the face').

387. Hecuba's sense of justice suggests that, since she is the mother of Paris, who killed Achilles, her death might be regarded as just compensation. She believes in vengeance, and she thinks it natural that the dead man should want blood-offerings. That is a touch important for her character in the sequel.

395. Odysseus, though obstinate in his policy, is not a mere ruffian.

396. Prayers having failed, Hecuba speaks like a Queen, commanding Odysseus to accept her as the substitute: Odysseus promptly reminds her of her helplessness. But she is prepared to make a hopeless effort by clinging to her child. At 402 it looks as if a struggle is beginning. Polyxena beautifully intervenes to prevent it, thinking, as always, of her mother's dignity, not of herself. In the litany of farewell that follows, Hecuba thinks mainly of her own sorrows, Polyxena of Hecuba's loneliness. Her references to Cassandra and Polydorus are meant to strengthen Hecuba. They are doubly pathetic, because, in the sequel, Hecuba will sacrifice her feelings about Cassandra to her vengeance for Polydorus, only to learn at the end that Cassandra, too, will be the victim of a woman's vengeance. Similarly, the savage cry for vengeance on the wanton Helen, which Hecuba utters, just before she faints, is a sudden revelation of her spirit. The contrast between Polyxena, who turns tragedy into beauty, and dies happy, and Hecuba, crying for vengeance, is essential to the plot of the whole play.

425. τῆς τύχης depends on ἀθλία, 'wretched for your . . .'

426. χαῖρε. Our own 'good-bye' is short for 'God be with ye', and is like the French 'adieu'. The Greek word for good-bye means properly 'rejoice', and the Latin vale, 'be healthy'; and the Russian 'presti' means 'pardon me'. Hecuba feels that χαῖρε has a bitter irony for her; as for Cassandra, her fate makes the irony even greater.

429. γ', 'Yes'.   πάντα, in everything, adverbial accusative.

430. θανούσης, 'when you die'.   τὸ σόν implies σοῦ.

437. We should say 'between this place and the sword &c.', whereas Greek leaves out 'this place' and simply says " ξίφους μεταξύ . . ." (cf. ἐν μέσῳ ἀήρ ἐστι γῆς, 'the atmosphere is in between the earth—and the heaven ').

441. ὥς accented = οὕτως.

Διοσκόροιν. Castor and Pollux, like Helen, were the children of Zeus and Leda.

442. εἷλε, destroyed, ruined. This pun on Helen's name is

frequent in tragedy. The Greeks thought names might really make a difference to people's character and fortune. Ajax—Αἴας—was so named by his father that he might be royal and strong like the eagle (αἰετός) : but when his life ended in shame he realized that his name meant ' sorrow', from the cry αἰαῖ, 'Alas'.

445. ἅτε, 'Thou who . . .': ignore τε in translating.

448. τῷ = τίνι. The dative goes with κτηθεῖσα, which is passive, and means 'having been made a possession of . . .' Slaves were regarded as the private property (κτήματα) of their masters (οἱ κεκτημένοι).

450. Supply πρός from the last sentence to govern ὅρμον. ' To a haven in the Dorian land?' i.e. the Peloponnese, land of Agamemnon and Menelaus.

451. Supply αἴας, 'or the land of Pthia', i.e. Thessaly, the land of Achilles. The river Apidanus flowed through a fertile valley in this country.

455. I have tried to translate this stanza and the next closely, in a rhythm like that of the original : these lines correspond metrically to 445-54 and 466-74 to 475-83. The whole ode represents the sad musing of the prisoners, wondering where they will be taken. It should be sung very softly, with graceful, quiet movements. The effect is to divide the first main episode from the second without letting the audience break away from the spell of the poetry. This quiet interlude after Hecuba's curse and collapse, is very effective. After wondering whether they will go to Argos, Sparta, or Thessaly, the women think of countries dearer to Athenians, first the sacred island of Delos—where the Ionians worshipped Apollo, and the treasury of the Delian League had been kept. Probably it was just before this play that the Athenians purified Delos and renewed the ancient festival of Apollo with fresh magnificence. Apollo was supposed to have been born there, and the sacred palm-tree to which Leto clung when she bore him was still shown to worshippers. It was at a shrine of Artemis (935) that the women had taken refuge on the night of the sack of Troy.

Finally, they think, perhaps it may be their lot to go to Athens, and help to make the robe offered to Athene in the Panathenaic festival, the greatest religious ceremony of the year. This was embroidered with the story of Athene's triumph, when she wielded the thunderbolt of Zeus against the Giants, who were fighting the gods, and overthrew them. The fate of the defeated Giants suggests to the Chorus that of their own country : so that the ode which had become more happy with the mention of Delos and Athens, ends, as it began, with sorrow. The last thought, as the music dies away, is the thought of their own humiliation, the same as the shame of Cassandra, which Polyxena is spared.

478. Ἀργείων possessive genitive after δορίκτητος.

482. ἀλλάξασα taking in exchange for Asia. θαλάμους in apposition to θεράπναν. Their home in Europe will be ' a bridal chamber of

Death' in the sense that it will be as bad as death, deadly: because it will be shameful.

484. δή ποτ' οὖσαν, 'she who once was, but now is not . . .'

486. If we say in English 'with her back on the ground', we suggest a picture of Hecuba lying on her back. That is not what the Greek phrase means: simply she is huddled up, with her back bent forward, crouching, so that what one sees is her back, which is thus 'on the ground'.

488. λέξω deliberative subjunctive 'What am I to say . . .?'

489. Translate 'Or that idly they hold this view, an opinion merely (ἄλλως), and a false one, when they think . . .' Many people at the time of Euripides doubted the existence of the gods. Thus Protagoras said, in a book which was burnt because it was thought impious, 'With respect to the gods I am unable to know either that they are or that they are not'. But the herald's thought is not philosophic, but natural. He sees the misery of Hecuba, and thinks 'Are there gods, or is everything just fortune?' It is interesting to note that in the next century Fortune was actually worshipped by many people as the most influential goddess. It is not Euripides, but the herald, in his dramatic character, who expresses this doubt. But for lines like this Euripides was thought a dangerous free-thinker.

498. Talthybius has that same thought which Polyxena expressed to Hecuba, 'better death than shame'.

513-14. These lines should be spoken by Hecuba to herself, very quietly. She is facing the fact that Polyxena is dead. Line 515 is spoken bravely, and with authority. There is a note of violence as she says 'With outrage . . .' It is a hint of her own character. The contrast with what follows is impressive.

524. Talthybius is much interested in his own office, which he thinks important, and also in the ritual. This is a touch of character, not overdone so as to be absurd. The effect of his careful recital of each detail is that we feel awed, with him, at the solemn service and the silence.

555-6. ὑστάτην ὄπα means 'the end of his words': οὗπερ depends on κείνου understood after ὄπα: translate 'because he was the person whose authority was supreme'. The stress laid on Agamemnon's authority, and every one's instant obedience, is (1) suited to the character of this very ceremonious herald, and (2) dramatic, since Agamemnon, if he had used his authority aright, might have prevented the whole tragedy. And in the sequel, he refuses justice to Hecuba, because he is afraid of the army.

558 ff. This exquisite picture of Polyxena is famous. Euripides probably had in mind the description of Iphigeneia's sacrifice in the *Agamemnon* of Aeschylus. 'They gagged her so that she could not speak: she let her bridal-veil of saffron fall to the ground about her, and with an eloquent pitiful glance her eye smote every one of the sacrificers, as she stood there, showing as in a picture, fain to speak to them.' Lucretius, who used the tale of Iphigeneia

as an illustration of the harm that has been done by superstition, represents the victim as less courageous :

> And soon as she was aware of her father standing
> Sorrowful by the altar, and at his side
> The priestly ministers hiding the knife,
> And the folk shedding tears at sight of her,
> Speechless in terror, dropping on her knees
> To the earth she sank down. [TREVELYAN.]

Ovid's Polyxena (*Metamorphoses* xiii) has a Roman courage; 'fortis et infelix et plusquam femina virgo'. 'The thought of my mother', she says, 'is the only thought which lessens my joy in death', 'quamvis | Non mea mors illi, verum sua vita gemenda est'. She bids them leave her free, 'Vos modo, ne Stygios adeam non libera manes, | Este procul... Priami vos filia regis, | Non captiva rogat': she does not weep, though the people, and even the priest, shed tears.

Swinburne's Chthonia, in *Erechtheus*, gives herself for Athens, and stands at the altar 'With light in all her face as of a bride | Smiling': her lips tremble, but 'with pride in pleasure that no fear blanched them': 'her cheeks | Lightened, and brighter than a bridal veil | Her hair enrobed her bosom, and enrolled | From face to feet the body's whole soft length | As with a cloud sun-saturate; then she spake | With maiden tongue words manlike, but her eyes | Lit mildly like a maiden's'.

559. Lit. 'to the waist at the level of the navel'. Translate simply 'right to the waist'.

562. τλημονέστατον means both brave and pitiful. 563-4. τόδε ... παῖσον, 'strike here'.

566. ''Twixt would and would not . . .'

568. καὶ θνῄσκουσα, 'though she was dying'.

569. English says 'Was very careful . . .'; Greek says 'Had much forethought . . .', to do so and so.

570. Lit. 'the things which'; translate 'all that it is right to hide from the eyes of men'.

571. σφαγή is the sacrificial stroke, cutting the throat. We should say 'the stroke was fatal, and she breathed away her life'.

572. Each had a different task, but all were busy.

574. When a victor returned from the Games, or a conqueror from war, the people would strew leaves on him, as we throw flowers or confetti. The people honoured Polyxena as a triumphant heroine.

576. 'Had to listen to reproaches like this . . .'

578. The offering of garments to the dead is a survival of the days when it was still thought that they wanted clothes and other mortal comforts in the grave. The Greeks pay Polyxena the honours that Homeric heroes give to their companions, and the Athenians to their own soldiers, who have fallen in war.

579. περισσά adverbial accusative neuter plural.

580. τοιάδ' repeats the τοιάδε of 576, and refers to the words just spoken : the construction, by a natural shift, makes λέγων nominative, as if the speaker of the words had been the subject of the sentence.

581–2. The order of the words in Greek makes this mean ' not only the most unfortunate, but also the most blest . . .'

583. The metaphor is from water rising, when it boils. We should say ' hath risen as a wave ', or something of that kind.

584. The Chorus attribute this tragedy to the inevitable destiny of the gods. Polyxena's heroism has made it possible for them to speak with calm resignation. Hecuba herself is strengthened by the thought of Polyxena's courage, and is able to be brave and calm herself, as Polyxena wished. She makes an effort, and succeeds in viewing her trouble as something outside herself. Her reflections are not, as some bad critics have said, irrelevant and undramatic : they are the result of a noble effort to keep her reason and her self-control.

587. τόδε, ' here is another which . . .'

588. Lit. ' following upon evils (gen.) with fresh evils '.

599. This thought is pathetic in view of the change which comes to Hecuba herself later on. She has brought up her children well and faithfully. That is a comfort to her now ; but she herself later on breaks down under the strain, and is made barbarous by the cruelty of Polymestor.

606. Hecuba's contempt and fear of democracy is again stressed. In the sequel she herself will be more violent and cruel than any mob. The port of the Peiraeus was notoriously radical and disorderly.

611. Had Polyxena lived to be a bride, her mother would have washed her in the sacred water of the river Scamander, and dressed her beautifully for marriage. Now she can only wash and anoint the body of this ' bride of Hades ', and make her beautiful for the funeral pyre.

628. κατ' ἦμαρ, ' day by day '. It is one of the chief maxims of Greek religion that mortals cannot look for perfect happiness : that is reserved for gods. We mortals are to be called happy, if, for the day, no great trouble comes to us. The end of Hecuba's speech has the beauty of the close of many Greek tragedies, when the sufferer is calm, and the audience, as Milton says, ' in peace and consolation ' is dismissed, ' and calm of mind, all passion spent '. Here the calm is the result of Polyxena's unselfishness, which has taken away the sting for Hecuba. There is no room left for thoughts of revenge. The scene is contrasted both with the first scene, which ended with a cry for vengeance, and with the later scenes of the play. The Chorus, in the same mood of reverent awe, sing with sorrow, but without bitterness, of Paris and Helen, and the troubles that came from their sin, ending, with a wonderful sympathy, in thoughts of the Spartan mothers who, like themselves, are grieving for the children. When we remember that this play

was written during the Peloponnesian war, and that the Spartans are not only the ancient enemies of Troy, but living foes of Athens, we feel the full beauty of this quiet close. The perfect scene, in which sorrow becomes beautiful, is sharply broken by the return of the Serving-woman, clamouring for Hecuba.

629. The repeated χρῆν ' it was fated, it was fated ' has the same effect as the reference to destiny in line 584. See the note there. ' For me too it was destiny, for me too it was fate, that decreed calamity and sorrow . . .'

635. τάν is relative. 'Who is the most beautiful of all the women whom . . .'

639–46. This stanza is the antistrophe, corresponding metrically to the strophe, 629–38. Lines 649 ff. are an 'Epode', i.e. a third stanza of different metrical shape, concluding the poem.

646. The herdsman was Paris, who gave the prize of beauty to Aphrodite, goddess of love, in return for her promise of Helen. The defeated goddesses were Hera and Athene.

650. Eurotas is the river of Sparta.

677. Once more by a skilful touch the poet reminds us of Cassandra.

684–8. Having realized at last that her son is dead, Hecuba feels the first onset of a strange wild passion. It is the spirit of revenge, driving her to madness. She resists at first. But it will change into a settled hate, inhuman and ruthless, when she realizes that the murderer is Polymestor. At lines 689 ff., after the first spasm of frenzy, she is comparatively calm, but shaken with sobs. She does not yet connect the death of the boy with Polymestor. At 698 the Serving-woman, by saying that she found the body on the sea-shore, gives her a clue : she remembers what her dream told her. (The prologue was her dream : see note on 30.) Hence her question at 699 f. Had he been cast out to the waves, or had he fallen in fight with an enemy on the sands? If he was thrown up by the waves, her dream was true, and Polymestor is the murderer.

705. τάν is relative, and follows ὄψιν (οὔ με παρέβα φάσμα μελανόπτερον being a parenthesis).

709. By the knowledge that your dream gives you . . .'

710. ἐμός emphatic: ' My own friend, my own friend . . .'

711. ἵνα, 'where', depends on the notion ' in Thrace' contained in Θρήκιος.

717. ' Cursed among men.'

726–7. ' Why do you delay to come and bury your child, accord· ing to the message which Talthybius brought me '. ἐφ' οἷς = ἐπὶ τούτοις ἅ.

731. ἐκεῖθεν, ' there '; i.e. at the place of the funeral (used for ἐκεῖ because it is the place *from which* he has just come).

734. ' That he is no Argive . . .'

770. Hecuba says this line slowly, so that Agamemnon may him- self think, before she says it, that Polymestor is guilty. Her mention of the gold in 772, serves the same purpose. But Agamemnon in

773, though he is ready to believe her, waits for her definite charge. He behaves as a weak man making a show of strength. He accepts her unsupported word at 776, then makes a show of being an impartial judge. His question at 779 'Why did you send her there? To search for the body?' is like that of a cross-examining barrister. Her answer, unexpected and pathetic, reminds him of her recent sorrow. There is a pause, and he admits that she is probably right. But a stronger man, with more respect for justice, would not so easily admit it. He would investigate the matter.

784. This line is tragic because we know that she has much more suffering to come.

793 ff. Three things make the crime worse: (1) Polymestor was Hecuba's friend, had sat at her table, been reckoned 'in the count of friendship' among the first, and always been treated properly: (2) he killed deliberately, to get the gold: (3) he did not bury the body.

800. 'It is because of Law that we think the gods exist.' The idea is that men's belief in the gods is based on the fact that the world is orderly, a kosmos not a chaos.

νόμῳ goes with both parts of the sentence, 'and it is because of Law that we live with justice and injustice marked off from each other': i. e. 'recognize in our lives a distinction between right and wrong'. Hecuba's appeal is to the lofty view that human Law and Justice are framed on the model of a divine Law, which governs the world, and, for instance, keeps the sun and moon and stars in their courses, and, above all, brings retribution for wrong. This Law, divine and human, now 'rests with Agamemnon', as the victorious king. If he betrays the trust, the Law itself will be betrayed. If the rulers of the world do not punish treachery and impiety, there will be no Justice among men, i. e. the world will no longer conform to the divine scheme.

801. ὁρίζω σοὶ τὰ δίκαια would mean 'I define for you, mark out for you, the things that are right': turn this into the passive, and you get "ὥρισμαι τὰ δίκαια", 'I have what is right marked out for me'.

802. The Law now comes to Agamemnon, demanding that this case shall be dealt with justly: if he refuses, he will, as it were, 'destroy the Law'.

804. φέρειν, 'violate'. The metaphor rose from the notion of carrying off sacred property, as plunder, but the phrase comes to mean simply sacrilege, or even any gross wickedness.

806. 'Regarding this, then, as a thing which would disgrace yourself' (i. e. neglect of the law, &c.) 'respect my prayer.' αἰσχύνη is the feeling that makes a man ashamed to do a thing because other people will condemn him: αἰδώς is a feeling that makes him ashamed to do it, because he himself feels it shameful. She appeals to Agamemnon to respect his reputation, and to follow his better feelings. Finally, she appeals to his pity.

807. A painter stands back from his picture to view it. She begs Agamemnon to view the picture of her misery. The phrase she uses, however, just hints that Agamemnon is in fact responsible, as the man who overthrew Troy.

812. Neither the appeal to abstract right, nor the appeal for pity, succeeds. Agamemnon turns away at line 811. Hecuba speaks lines 813 ff. half to herself. They mark the transition from the lofty tone of 798 ff. to a fresh and shameful appeal. Agamemnon by refusing justice, drives her on to a terrible moral humiliation. He thus becomes responsible for the results.

με is governed by the idea (φεύγεις or the like) implied in ὑπεξάγεις πόδα (lit. withdraw your foot).

814. At all costs Hecuba feels she must win the King. She unsays what she has always said in the past. As a queen, and also as a women of high intelligence, she has hated the rhetoricians and their tricks. Now, in her desperate situation, she bitterly admits that the rhetorician's art, the trick of persuasion, is worth more than any other sort of knowledge. She casts about for some fresh argument (821 ff.), then at last forces herself to exploit her daughter's shame.

816. There is a reminder here of her previous appeal to law. She bitterly owns that not the law of right, but only Persuasion, is the ruler of men : and the rule is not lawful, but a lawless despotism.

817. οὐδέν τι μᾶλλον, 'none the more for that', i. e. its enormous influence does not make us any the more study it ἐς τέλος, thoroughly.

818. Lit. 'in order that it might have been in our power'. The idiom is regular since the meaning is practically 'I wish we had learnt it, in order that we might . . . : but we haven't'. βούλοιτο in the next line is the regular optative in a general relative sentence in the past 'to plead any cause one wished, and succeed in it'.

823. τόνδε, 'yonder'. She points towards the sea, as if Troy were actually visible across the straits.

824 ff. This tragic moment of humiliation is the turning-point of Hecuba's moral tragedy. Polyxena's wish that she should be spared shame, is not fulfilled. But she sees that she has made an effect on Agamemnon, and lines 832 ff. are spoken confidently. She claims that Polydorus, as the brother of Cassandra, is a kinsman of the King. All the allusions to Cassandra's fate which we have noted have been the preparation for this climax.

835. Agamemnon still hesitates. For the moment Hecuba fears that she has failed. She desperately searches for another argument. The violent rhetoric of 836 ff. would be absurd if it were not the result of the great emotional crisis through which she has passed, in forcing herself to speak as she has about Cassandra. She is suffering and distracted. Finally, she finishes the act of abasement by hailing Agamemnon, the destroyer of her country, as 'the Light of Greece'. Until line 841, Hecuba, Queen of Troy, has never addressed Agamemnon, or any man, as Master.

845. The final couplet states the crude law of vengeance on which Hecuba herself will act. When this play was composed, the best minds, like that of Socrates, were denying its validity. 'Honour the gods, your parents, strangers, and the laws', said the old Greek morality: but also 'Do harm to your enemies by all possible means'. The old law of vengeance was 'an eye for an eye', &c. But Socrates, and those who, like Euripides, thought with him, believed in a higher law, which bids us do good to enemies as well as friends, because if we harm an enemy we really harm ourselves.

846 ff. Morally there is still hope. Agamemnon can save everything by bringing Polymestor to fair trial. The Chorus still under the impression made by Hecuba's appeal to Law, find a confirmation in the spectacle of Hecuba and Agamemnon. 'Strange', they say, 'how all things conspire together, in human lives: there are surely laws which determine destiny'—i. e. we are not creatures of blind chance, and fate moves in accordance with law. It is, they think, an example of the working of divine law, overruling all the chances of human life, that Hecuba and Agamemnon, once enemies, should now be joined together in the work of justice against Polymestor, once Hecuba's friend, but now a traitor. Agamemnon's answer shows that he has not courage to play the high part which is still possible for him. For the bad reason of his passion for Cassandra, he is willing to connive in Hecuba's vengeance: for the bad reason that he fears public opinion, he is not willing to take the responsibility himself.

850. Agamemnon mentions in turn each of the pleas advanced by Hecuba: he respects her as a suppliant, and pities her misfortune: he wishes, for the sake of the gods and justice, that Polymestor should be punished. But for all that, he will take no responsibility. He would like to help, but will not do anything which might annoy the Greeks.

864. Hecuba, the slave, suddenly sees that Agamemnon the King is himself not free—his character makes him a slave to public opinion and private passion. In this fine speech she herself throws off all allegiance to Law. The law will not help her: very well, she will act for herself, as an outlaw fighting her own fight. There is a splendid irony in her assurance (869) 'since you are afraid, I will make you free from this fear'.

867. Lit. 'check' or 'hamper him, so that he uses ways of behaviour not in accordance with his judgement'.

868. 'Make too much of . . .', lit. 'give too much to . . .'

870. 'Connive', lit. 'share my knowledge . . .'

873. 'The kind of thing he shall suffer' is very grim. φανῇ is aorist passive, and goes with θόρυβος and ἐπικουρία: 'if there arise a disturbance . . . or if a rescue is attempted . . .', we should say.

874. 'Check it for my sake, though not appearing to do it for my sake.'

875. The last words, 'I will order all things well', are a quotation from the end of Aeschylus' *Agamemnon*. Clytaemnestra, having killed her husband, desperately hopes that with Aegisthus she may turn a new leaf, and live a good life: as she leads Aegisthus into the palace, she says, 'You and I, as rulers, will order all things well'. The audience knows that the wish is hopeless. This grim reminiscence adds point to the following little scene, in which Agamemnon makes so light of what women can do. The whole scene in which Hecuba persuades Agamemnon to connive at her plot recalls the great scene of the temptation of Agamemnon by Clytaemnestra in Aeschylus.

883. 'Why how . . . ?' κράτος means 'victory'.

885. μέμφομαι, 'I make little account of . . .' When he gets home, Agamemnon will discover his mistake: women are weak, but, as Hecuba says, 'difficult to fight against, when cunning is their weapon'.

887. These famous instances of great crimes committed by women are cited by the Chorus in Aeschylus' *Choephoroe*, when they reflect on Clytaemnestra's crime, and its impending punishment. The fifty daughters of Danaus killed their husbands, the sons of Aegyptus, except one, who was spared by the heroic Hypermestra. When the Argonauts came to Lemnos, they found that all the men had been murdered by their wives.

889. 'Give me safe conduct for this woman . . .' It is the old Serving-woman. Hecuba says γυναῖκα ironically, with reference to Agamemnon's contempt for what women can do.

892. χρέος adverbial accusative 'in a matter which concerns you not less than her'.

896. Greek stresses the first words in the sentence, which runs down at the end. So the meaning here is 'That these two, brother and sister, may be buried, near each other, burnt in one flame . . .'

902. 'May some good end it.' Agamemnon expressed just the same sort of vague hope that all will end well, when he decided to sacrifice Iphigeneia. He is a kind of Micawber in small matters, and tragically like Pontius Pilate in great, always talking about virtue, and washing his hands of responsibility.

905. Before reading this chorus, it will be well to notice how perfectly the musical interludes suit the atmosphere and movement of the play. First, the pathetic musical scene of Hecuba, Polyxena, and the Chorus at the beginning. Then, after Polyxena was taken away, and Hecuba had cursed Helen, the Chorus sang an ode about their future fate in Greece, ending with thoughts of the shameful lot which awaited them instead of marriage. At the centre, after the description of Polyxena's noble death, when Hecuba was calm, and grief turned to beauty, the choral ode, though it remembered Helen and Paris, the fatal bride and bridegroom, ended with thoughts of sympathy for enemy brides and mothers. In the next part, a short and more violent musical scene, between Hecuba and the Serving-woman, marked the change in Hecuba's feeling when she discovered

Polymestor's treachery. Now, when her plot for vengeance is laid, the Chorus sing a splendid ode, about their last night in Troy, as happy brides, their vain appeal to the gods, and finally, the violent curse on Helen with which they sailed as prisoners bound for Greece. The last lyrical scene will be the most violent of all, and Polymestor will be the soloist. It is highly dramatic that the Chorus, catching something of Hecuba's mood, should picture all the past wrongs now, and end with a curse on Helen.

953 ff. With the curse on Helen still ringing in our ears, we come to the great scene of Hecuba's vengeance. Polymestor, magnificently clad and fully armed, arrives with the two young princes, and with a body-guard of Thracian soldiers, in barbaric costume. Thus the spectacle is becoming more and more sumptuous. It will reach its climax in the last scene, when Agamemnon with a body-guard of the Greek army, will fill up the picture.

Polymestor overdoes his part, by invoking Priam, as if he were still alive.

956 ff. The hypocrite professes to hold a creed the opposite of that to which Hecuba appealed while she was still hoping for justice. She said 'We believe in the gods, because there is law in the world': Polymestor says—little knowing what awaits him—'There is nothing we can trust . . . the gods make a chaos of everything, in order that in ignorance we may worship them'. Hecuba herself is now acting as if the world were such a chaos. Her vengeance goes far beyond justice. It recoils upon herself.

958. 'The gods themselves stir and confuse everything'—like the ingredients of a pudding (Walpole).

959. ἀγνωσίᾳ, because we do not know what may happen in such a confused world.

961. προκόπτοντα is masculine and agrees with the subject (understood) of θρηνεῖν. The meaning is 'Why should one lament, since by lamenting one does not make any headway in dealing with one's troubles'.

962. 'If you blame me at all for staying away from you . . .' He might have been expected to come at once, on hearing that she had been brought to Thrace.

963. τυγχάνω. Translate 'I happened to be away'. The present is vivid in Greek.

965. English would put the participle as a main verb, thus: 'After I had arrived home, I was already starting . . . when your servant met me . . .'

968 ff. Hecuba dare not look at Polymestor, for fear she should show the hate in her eyes. She pretends that a sense of disgrace at the contrast between her misery and her former greatness is the cause. She appealed to Agamemnon's αἰσχύνη and αἰδώς. In her changed mood she is ready to make bitter play with these words.

970. ὅτῳ goes with σέ in 973.

973. Her ironical apology is a retort to his pretence that his failure to visit her had been due to no lack of friendship.

974. The climax of irony is reached when she pretends that she—who has determined to throw over all restraints of 'law'—refrains from looking at him because 'it is the custom' for women modestly to avoid the eyes of men. Polymestor's reply, 'And no marvel', though he only means 'no wonder you are so much overcome', is for the audience pointed, in view of what Hecuba is really planning.

976. σ' governed by ἔχει, which is commonly left out in this phrase.

977. Do not translate πόδα literally. The meaning is ' Why did you send for me to come here?'

978. δή emphasizes ἴδιον ἐμαυτῆς, ' It is a private matter of my own that I wish to tell you and your sons . . .'

983. χρῆν makes the sentence mean 'you ought to be telling me, though you are not telling'.

986. The construction of παῖδα is like the famous οἶδα σὲ τίς εἶ, ' I know thee who thou art'. ' First tell me of the son . . . whether . . .'

989. 'Certainly, so far as he is concerned' (μέρος adverbial accusative).

992. τι, ' at all '.

993. γε, ' yes '; καί, ' and '. Notice the order of the words, always used in this sort of answer. ὡς σέ, ' to you ': this use of ὡς is generally with persons.

994. Our idiom says ' which he had with him when he came '.

996. ἔρα, ' become enamoured of your neighbours' property '.

997. ' No, no. My prayer is only to enjoy what I already have.' The hypocrite uses pious phrases about freedom from covetousness. But both here and at 995 his words fit the facts he is trying to conceal.

1022. The irony of the last line is effective. An actor playing Polymestor would start with a guilty conscience, and hesitate : then he would shrug his shoulders, reflecting that her words meant nothing, and go in. The moment the door has closed, the Chorus begin to chant their grim little song. But even they have not realized to what lengths Hecuba means to go. They are horrified when they hear that the children are murdered. They had expected only Polymestor's death. But they forget their horror in fear for Hecuba and the Trojan women, when the Thracian is heard battering at the walls.

1035. There is a moment's silence : then suddenly the cry of Polymestor is heard. The effect is like that of the *Agamemnon*, when the King's cry οἴμοι πέπληγμαι is heard from the palace. So, in his second cry, Agamemnon says οἴμοι μάλ' αὖθις.

1037. σφαγῆς depends on ὤμοι, ' Alas for your miserable murder '.

1038. καινά means ' terrible and unexpected '. So at 689 Hecuba had called the murder of her son ἄπιστα, καινά, καινά.

1039. οὐ μή with aorist subjunctive expresses a strong denial ' You shall not any way escape '.

1040 ff. Probably one of the Chorus-leaders utters the first cry, and another calls to the rest to break in and rescue Hecuba.

1044. The Thracian is blindly battering at the walls, which he has mistaken for the gates. Hecuba is able to slip out, and leaves the doors open. Her voice is heard at 1044 taunting the Thracian, and at 1046 she appears. κρατεῖς means 'are you victor' (ξένον going closely with Θρῆκα, and the καὶ κρατεῖς being slipped in as an excited parenthesis).

1053. ὅδε, 'here': she points to the open doors.

1055. θυμῷ ζέοντι dative depending on δυσμαχωτάτῳ, 'an evil enemy to face with his wrath boiling'.

1056 ff. The whole monody is a terrible sequel to the monody of Hecuba at the beginning of the play. Just as Hecuba was heard lamenting within, then came out into the sunlight, so the Thracian rages at first helplessly in the hut, then gropes his way out, and (at 1067) emerges into the full light. He feels the warmth, and pathetically appeals to the Sun-god.

1057. 'Where am I to step? Where can I stand? Where am I to come to rest? (κέλσω)': the metaphor is of a ship coming to land. This image is taken up again at the end of the song. It is important to realize that this is a musical composition, with calmer moments between bursts of fury. The Thracian is a savage, and even talks of eating the flesh of the murderous women; but also he feels, and makes us feel, for the children. He is alternately furious and desolate.

1058. This is heard, not seen. He has ceased to batter the walls, and is crawling about the hut trying to catch the women. βάσιν τιθέμενος is equivalent to βαίνων, 'moving with the gait of a four-footed beast', and ἐπίχειρα is an adverbial accusative 'on my hands'. κατ᾽ ἴχνος means 'on the trail' of my prey.

1059-60. 'Which way shall I turn aside': lit. 'which road, this or that, shall I choose instead' (of my present one).

1065. The effect of the word κατάρατοι here is very great, because it is the climax of a series of cursings (see 166, 441 ff., and especially 716 and 945).

1069. 'Giving me light instead' of darkness. At this moment the other women slip out of the hut, and he hears them passing him. He is carried away by fury, and becomes a raving cannibal. Then, failing to catch them, he suddenly feels that he has left his children's bodies at the mercy of these creatures. He gropes his way back to the door, and in the tableau thus formed, with the Thracian in the centre, and the orchestra thronged with Hecuba and the women, the scene is set for the return of Agamemnon.

1077. 'Bacchants of Death': the reference is to the frenzied worshippers of Dionysus, who tear and eat the bodies of animals. These strange rites, which had been long abandoned in civilized Athens, persisted in the savage northern regions, like Thrace. It was in Thrace that Orpheus, the poet, was said to have been torn to pieces by women. With the return to the metaphor of a ship (see 1057) the music becomes calmer, and pathos takes the place of horror. At 1089, with the sudden call for help, first to the Thracian guards, then to the Greeks, the whole scene changes again to action.

1100. This is the finest moment in the musical scene. The Thracian is a monster : he is also a human being, longing for peace. But, if he flies to the heaven, there are the fiery shafts of the Dog-star and of Orion—the most brilliant of the stars—to scorch him : if he goes down to Hell, there is darkness. The Chorus have become awed, and almost sympathetic. Their words at 1107–8 come quietly, with a touch of consolation. Death is the end. But neither the Thracian nor Hecuba are ready for it. The sordid treachery of the one, the cruel vengeance of the other, have brought them to a level, in everything except intelligence, below common humanity. Now, in the last debate, they fight for Agamemnon's verdict with their wits.

1109. Agamemnon enters in state, attended. The pageant is now complete. His high-flown language covers the fact that he really knows at any rate the chief fact that he pretends to ask about. We despise his pretence, and can have no respect for his verdict.

οὐ and ἥσυχος go together ' with no peaceful voice . . .'

1113. παρέσχεν, ' would have caused '. The sense is exactly as if we had ἄν. This use is rare, but not ungrammatical, and reminds us of Horace's famous tree—' me truncus illapsus cerebro | sustulerat nisi Faunus ictum | dextra levasset '.

1122. σὺ . . . σύ emphatic, expressing surprise that Hecuba could have done such a thing. These words show Polymestor that Hecuba is present. He falls into a fit of fury, but is restrained by the King.

1127. οὗτος contemptuous, ' Sirrah ! ' Agamemnon signs to his guard to seize the Thracian.

1128. ' Let me go, that I may . . .'

1135. ' You see, he had a presentiment that Troy would fall.' The δή is for Agamemnon's benefit, and the sentence is meant to prejudice him. The vivid subjunctives in 1139 have a similar effect : they tend to make the alleged danger more real. ' I feared— he may gather Troy together, and found a city with the remnant, and then, I thought, the Greeks might . . .'

1144. νῦν, ' in the present war '. ἐκάμνομεν, ' we were troubled '. Thucydides held that during the siege of Troy the Greeks supported themselves by plunder and by farming the Chersonese. Poly-mestor's argument, though fraudulent, is plausible, and must have struck the audience as a typical specimen of the unscrupulous attempts to justify crimes in the name of patriotism, which were common in the Peloponnesian war, as in all wars.

1153. Thracian needlework, especially brightly coloured gar-ments, decorated with patterns of animals, were famous. Thucydides gives an account of the great wealth of Sitalces, 400 talents in silver and gold coin, and ' gifts of no less value in gold and silver, besides embroidered and plain stuffs . . .' contributed to the kings and petty chiefs by their subjects. 'The principle of the Thracian noble—unlike that of the Persians—was to take, not give . . . You can get nothing out of them without a bribe.'

1187. Hecuba arranges her matter with all the skill of the orators, whom she used to despise. But morally, she is now a savage, like Polymestor. We remember that she, too, is a Thracian by birth, when she declares that Greeks and barbarians can never be friends; then, in the same breath, she hints to Agamemnon that she relies on him not to forget 'his kinsman' Polydorus. Her refutation of Polymestor is triumphantly convincing. She proceeds to torture him by showing what his greed has cost him. Finally, she turns to Agamemnon, almost threatening, for his verdict, then, with a final stroke of feminine ingenuity, breaks off, with the flattering conclusion, 'I will not criticize my Master'. Remember how difficult she once found it to use that title.

1211. εἴπερ, 'since, as you say, . . .'

1214. Notice the tense: 'now when we are . . .' In the next line the aorist means 'the city, by its smoke, told you as much'. πολεμίων ὕπω is used as if she had said 'we are utterly destroyed'.

1227. αὐτά, 'of its own accord', good fortune (ἕκαστα, lit. on each occasion) 'always'. Luck never lacked a friend.

1234. 'Faithful to those to whom he ought to have been faithful.'

1237. τοιοῦτον ὄντα, 'because you are like them . . . bad'.

1240. Agamemnon is anxious to show that there is no collusion.

1243. ἐμὴν χάριν, 'for my sake': οὔτ' οὖν Ἀχαίων, 'nor for the sake of the Greeks either . . .'

1248. How sensitive Agamemnon professes to be to the Greek 'honour'! Yet he did not yield to this plea when Hecuba urged it.

1249. His character again. Even now, he puts his decision on the ground that he must avoid criticism.

1254 ff. The verdict has been given in favour of Hecuba. But her victim has still a word to say. He knows a secret of the future, and he uses it, as his last weapon. The prophecy that she will turn into a mad dog does not put too much strain on the imagination, for we have seen her moral transformation already. This dreadful crouching figure, with hate in its eyes, has already become less than human. Hecuba receives the news with indifference. Polymestor cannot hurt her: 'I do not care, since you have paid the penalty'. That is the climax of her triumph. Polymestor's answer changes the whole situation. He tells her that Cassandra, the daughter whose dishonour she has used as a pawn in the game of vengeance, is to die. She tries not to believe him. He repeats it: the wife of Agamemnon will kill her. Hecuba's last words are a wild prayer that the Tyndarid woman—Helen's sister—'may not be smitten with such madness'. The doctrine of revenge has recoiled on Hecuba herself. In Cassandra's fate, Polymestor will be avenged.

After that Hecuba remains transfixed, in tragic silence. Agamemnon may bluster, and order the Thracian to a desert island: the Trojan women are marshalled for the voyage to captivity. But we see Hecuba still, hardly human, on the brink of the final transformation, yet human enough to feel the sting of this last, worst grief.

1267. Herodotus tells us of the Satrai, who lived on the snow-capped mountains of Thrace, free, independent, and warlike. ' These are the owners of the famous oracle of Dionysus.... The interpreters of the shrine are a branch of the Satrai called Bessoi, and the prophetess is a priestess, who gives the oracles, just as at Delphi, and in no way more subtly'. He is defending the Delphic oracle against people who thought that the oracle of the Thracian Dionysus was even more wonderful.

VOCABULARY

ἀγαθός, -ή, -όν, good.
ἄγαλμα, -ατος, τό, statue.
Ἀγαμέμνων, -ονος, ὁ, Agamemnon, king of Mycenae.
ἀγαστός, -ή, -όν, desirable, worth living.
ἀγγέλλω, ἀγγελῶ, ἤγγειλα, announce, report, indicate.
ἀγέραστος, -ον, with no gift of honour.
ἄγκυρα, ἡ, anchor, sheet-anchor.
ἀγνωσία, ἡ, ignorance.
ἄγρα, ἡ, the chase, prey, spoil.
ἄγω, ἄξω, ἤγαγον, lead, take, spend.
ἀγών, -ῶνος, ὁ, conflict, struggle.
ἀγωνία, ἡ, conflict.
ἀδελφός, ὁ, brother.
ἀδικέω, am unjust to, wrong, do a wrong.
ἄδικος, -ον, wrong-doing, wrong.
ἀδοξέω, am held in no esteem.
ἀεί, adv. always.
ἄθλιος, -α, -ον and -ος, -ον, wretched, unhappy.
ἄθραυστος, -ον, unbroken, still standing.
ἀθροίζω, gather together.
ἄθροισις, -εως, ἡ, a gathering, mustering.
αἶα, ἡ, land.
αἰαῖ, exclamation of grief, alas! woe is me!
Αἴγυπτος, ὁ, King Aegyptus, whose fifty sons were put to death by their brides.

αἰδέομαι, -έσομαι, feel shame or respect, have regard for.
Ἅιδης, -ου, ὁ, the unseen world, the lord of the Under World.
αἰδώς, -οῦς, ἡ, a feeling of shame, self-respect.
αἷμα, -ατος, τό, blood, the shedding of blood.
αἱμάσσω, aor. ἤμαξα, stain with blood.
αἱματόεις, -εσσα, -εν, stained with blood, blood-reeking.
αἱρέω, -ήσω, εἷλον, seize, destroy, slay.
αἴρω, ἀρῶ, ἦρα, raise, fit out; αἴρειν πόδα, start.
αἰσθάνομαι, -ήσομαι, ᾐσθόμην, perceive, am aware of.
ἀΐσσω, ἀξω, ἤξα, move with swift gliding motion, hover.
αἰσχρός, -ά, -όν, shameful, discreditable, base; αἰσχρῶς, shamefully.
αἰσχύνη, ἡ, dishonour, discredit.
αἰσχύνομαι, -οῦμαι, ᾐσχύνθην, am ashamed.
αἴτιον, τό, cause.
αἰχμαλωτίς, -ίδος, ἡ, captive.
αἰχμάλωτος, -ον, taken by the spear, prisoner of war.
ἀΐω, hear.
αἰωρέω, raise; pass. am suspended, hover.
ἄκατος, ἡ, ὁ, light vessel, ship.
ἀκέομαι, -έσομαι, ἠκεσάμην, heal.

ἄκλαυτος, -ον, unwept.

ἀκμή, ἡ, crisis.

ἀκούω, hear, listen ; ἀκούειν κακῶς or κακά, am ill spoken of, reproached.

ἄκρος, -α, -ον, topmost, extreme, top of, surface of ; οὐκ ἄκρας κ. ἔψαυσε, it made a deep impression.

ἀκτή, ἡ, shore.

ἀλγέω, am pained, distressed.

Ἀλέξανδρος, ὁ, Alexander, Paris, son of Priam and Hecuba.

ἀλίαστος, -ον, unabating, incessantly.

Ἅλιος, v. ἥλιος.

ἅλιος, -α, -ον or -ος, -ον, of the sea.

ἁλίσκομαι, ἀλώσομαι, ἑάλων, used as pass. of αἱρέω, am taken, captured.

ἀλκή, ἡ, strength, force.

ἀλλά, but.

ἀλλάσσω, ἀλλάξω, ἤλλαξα, change, give, or take, in exchange.

ἄλλος, -η, -ο, another, other ; οἱ ἄλλοι, all the rest, all others. ἄλλως, differently, otherwise, vainly, to no purpose.

ἄλλοτε, at other times, sometimes.

ἀλλότριος, -α, -ον, of another, of others.

ἅλς, ἁλός, ἡ, the sea.

ἅλωσις, -εως, ἡ, capture, conquest.

ἅμα, adv. at the same time.

ἀμήχανος, -ον, helpless, impossible, inconceivable.

ἄμιλλα, ἡ, contest, conflict.

ἄμορφος, -ον, misshapen, unsightly, unseemly.

ἀμφί, prep. c. acc., gen., dat. around, about, concerning, at.

ἀμφιτίθημι, -θήσω, -έθηκα, -έθην, put about, cover with.

ἄν, condit. particle not separately translated, used in the apodosis of a conditional sentence,

and in subj. clauses with ὅς, ὅτε, ἐπεί, &c.

ἀνά, prep. c. acc. up and down, throughout.

ἀναγκάζω, force, compel.

ἀνάγκη, ἡ, necessity ; σιτοποιὸς ἀνάγκη, the forced task of making bread.

ἀναθρέω, look up at, mark.

ἄναξ, -ακτος, ὁ, king.

ἀναρρήγνυμι, -ρήξω, shatter, burst through.

ἄνασσα, ἡ, queen.

ἀνδροφόνος, -ον, man-slaying, murderous.

ἀνεκτός, -όν, tolerable.

ἀνέρχομαι, -ελεύσομαι, -ῆλθον, come up, come before, present oneself to.

ἀνήρ, ἀνδρός, ὁ, man.

ἀνθέω, bloom, flourish, wage victorious war.

ἄνθρωπος, ὁ, human being, man.

ἀνίστημι, -αναστήσω, ἀνέστησα (trans.) ; -έστην, -έστηκα and midd. (intrans.) raise ; am depopulated, laid waste.

ἀνόσιος, -ον, unholy, sinful.

ἀντί, prep. c. gen. instead of, in return for ; ἀνθ' ὅτου, the reason for which.

ἄνω, adv. above, in the world above.

ἀνωνόμαστος,-ον, not to be named, too horrible for words.

ἀξία, ἡ, worth, deserts, position.

ἄξιος, -α, -ον, worthy, deserving of ; ἀξίως, right worthily (with poetic irony).

ἀξιόω, deem worthy.

ἀξίωμα, -ατος, τό, esteem in which one is held, repute.

ἄπαις, ἄπαιδος, ὁ, ἡ, childless.

ἀπαλλάσσω, -αλλάξω, -ήλλαξα, set free, put away, loose one's hold of.

ἅπας, ἅπασα, ἅπαν, all, the whole.

ἄπειμι, -έσομαι, -ῆν, am absent, am away.

ἄπειμι, *used as fut. of* ἀπέρχομαι,
I will go away.

'Απιδανός, ὁ, a river in Thessaly,
flowing into the Peneus.

ἀπιστέω, have no confidence,
doubt, mistrust.

ἀπό, *prep. c. gen.* from.

ἀπόβλεπτος, -ον, conspicuous,
attracting every eye.

ἀποκτείνω, -κτενῶ, -έκτεινα, slay.

ἄπολις, -ι, having no city *or*
country, cityless.

ἀπόλλυμι, -ολέσω *and* -ολῶ,
-ώλεσα, destroy, bring to
death *or* ruin; *midd.* I am
undone, ruined, slain.

ἀποξενόω, drive from home, exile.

ἀποσπάω, -σπάσω, -έσπασα, drag
away from.

ἀποστέλλω, -στελῶ, -έστειλα, send
away, hasten departure.

ἀπουσία, ἡ, absence.

ἅπτομαι, ἅψομαι, ἡψάμην, touch,
cling to, support.

ἀπωθέω, -ώσω, -έωσα, thrust away;
midd. reject.

ἄρα, then, so then, *generally
implying that a previous con-
viction is confirmed.*

ἀράσσω, strike furiously.

'Αργεῖος, -α, -ον, Argive.

ἄργυρος, ὁ, silver, money.

ἄρδην, *adv.* = ἀέρδην, raised aloft,
utterly.

ἀριθμός, ὁ, number.

ἄριστος, -η, -ον, *superl. of* ἀγαθός,
best, most excellent, most
noble.

ἀρκέω, ἀρκέσω, ἥρκεσα, aid, succour.

ἀρνέομαι, deny, disown, gainsay.

ἁρπάζω, snatch, seize.

ἄρρητος, -η, -ον *and* -ος, -ον, not
to be spoken, too horrible for
words.

ἄρσην, ἄρσεν, male; ἄρσενες, men.

ἀρτίως, *adv.* just now.

ἀσθενής, -ές, weak, helpless.

'Ασία, ἡ, Asia.

ἄστυ, -εως, τό, city.

ἀσφαλής, -ές, safe; ἐν ἀσφαλεῖ,
in safety; ἀσφαλῶς, safely.

ἄταφος, -ον, unburied.

αὖ, *adv.* again.

αὐγάζω, beam upon, look upon
with beams.

αὐδή, αὐδά, ἡ, voice.

αὖθις, *adv.* again, once more.

αὐλή, ἡ, dwelling, abode.

αὐξάνω, make great; αὔξομαι,
imperf. ηὐξόμην, grow, thrive.

αὔρα, ἡ, breeze.

αὐτίκα, *adv.* presently, immedi-
ately.

αὐτός, -ή, -ό, self; *in oblique
cases a weak demonstr.* = eum,
eam, id; ὁ αὐτός, the same.

αὐχήν, -ένος, ἡ, neck, throat.

ἀφίημι, -ήσω, -ῆκα, -ῆν, send away,
relinquish, leave, cast out;
ἀφιέναι πνεῦμα, breathe one's
last.

ἀφικνέομαι, -ίξομαι, -ικόμην, arrive
at, come to.

ἀφίστημι, ἀποστήσω, ἀπέστησα,
put away; -έστην, -έστηκα,
-εστάθην, *and all tenses of
midd.* stand away from, withdraw, retreat.

ἀφορμή, ἡ, starting-point, basis,
motive.

'Αχαϊκός, -ή, -όν, Achaean.

'Αχαιός, -ά, -όν, Achaean; 'Αχαιοί,
οἱ, Achaeans, Greeks.

ἀχθεινός, -ή, -όν, burdensome.

'Αχιλεύς, -έως, ὁ, Achilles, son of
Peleus and Thetis.

'Αχιλλεύς (*as above*).

'Αχίλλειος, -α, -ον, of Achilles.

ἄωρος, -ον, untimely.

βαίνω, βήσομαι, ἔβην, go, step.

βάλλω, βαλῶ, ἔβαλον, throw,
strike, strew.

βάρβαρος, -ον, barbarian, foreign;
τὸ βάρβαρον, savagery.

βαρύς, -εῖα, -ύ, heavy, oppressive,
violent.

βασιλεύς, -έως, ό, king.
βάσις, -εως, ή, gait, tread.
βέλος, -ους, τό, missile, blow.
βία, ή, force, violence.
βίος, ό, life, livelihood, means.
βλέπω, see, look upon, regard, look upon the light of day, live (*with or without* φῶς).
βλέφαρον, τό, eyelid, eye.
βλώσκω, μολοῦμαι, ἔμολον, come.
βούλευμα, -ατος, τό, purpose, high resolve.
βουλεύω, plan, scheme for.
βούλομαι, wish, am bent on, desire (*pass. aor.* ἐβουλήθην *in same sense*).
βραχίων, -ονος, ό, arm.
βροτός, ό, mortal man.
βωμός, ό, altar.

γαῖα, ή, land, ground.
γάμος, ό, marriage; γάμοι, 'my hand'.
γάρ, *conj.* for; *elliptic, with* 'yes' *or* 'no' *to be supplied from context.*
γε, *enclitic particle,* at least; *commonly it serves to emphasize preceding word.*
γείτων, -ονος, ό, ή, neighbour.
γένειον, τό, chin, beard.
γένος, -ους, τό, race.
γένυς, -υος, ή, the under jaw, cheek.
γεραιός, -ά, -όν, aged.
γέρων, -οντος, ό, old man.
γεύομαι, taste, have experience of.
γῆ, ή, land.
γηραιός, -ά, -όν, aged.
γίγνομαι, γενήσομαι, ἐγενόμην, γέγονα *and* γέγαα, am born, become.
γιγνώσκω, γνώσομαι, ἔγνων, recognize, know, acknowledge, learn.
γλῶσσα, ή, tongue.
γνώμη, ή, resolution, will; κατὰ γνώμην, according to one's mind.

γοερός, -ά, -όν, mournful.
γόνυ, γόνατος, τό, knee.
γόος, ό, lamentation.
γραῖα, ή, old woman; *as adj.* aged.
γραῦς, γραός, ή, old woman.
γραφεύς, -έως, ό, painter.
γραφή, ή, writing; νόμων γραφαί, the written law.
γυνή, -αικός, ή, woman.

δαίμων, -ονος, ό, ή, god, goddess, heavenly being.
δάκρυ, τό, tear.
δάκρυον, τό, tear.
δακρύω, weep.
δάμαρ, δάμαρτος, ή, wife.
Δαναοί, οἱ, Danaans, Greeks.
δέ, *conj.* but, and, now; μὲν ... δέ, on the one hand ... on the other; δ' οὖν, be that as it may.
δεῖ, δεήσει, *impers.* it is necessary; ἃ δεῖ, what is right.
δείδω, δείσομαι, ἔδεισα, fear.
δείκνυμι, δείξω, ἔδειξα, show, bare to view.
δεινός, -ή, -όν, dread, terrible, dangerous.
δέμας, τό, body, form.
δέσποινα, ή, mistress.
δεσπότης, -ου, ό, master, lord.
δεῦρο, *adv.* hither.
δεύτερος, -α, -ον, second; δεύτορον, in the second place, afterwards, next.
δή, *a particle used generally to emphasize the word preceding it,* indeed, in truth, pray.
δηκτήριος, -ον, biting, torturing.
δῆτα, *adv., in questions marks a difference,* πῶς δῆτα, how then? τί δῆτα, what, pray? *in answers it echoes a word just used; it strengthens negatives.*
διά, *prep. c. gen.* through, by means of; *c. acc.* through, owing to.

διάδοχος, ὁ, ἡ, successor, bringing a succession of.

διαμοιράω, διαμοιράομαι, slash.

διασπάω, διασπάσομαι, rend asunder, tear limb from limb.

δίαυλος, ὁ, double channel; δίαυλοι, ebb and flow.

διαφθείρω, -φθερῶ, -έφθειρα, fut. pass. διαφθαρήσομαι, destroy, impair.

διδάσκω, διδάξω, ἐδίδαξα, teach, explain, advise.

δίδωμι, δώσω, ἔδωκα (paradigm, δός, δῶ, δοίην, δοῦναι, δούς), give, make.

διεργάζομαι, make an end of, slay.

δίκα, δίκη, ἡ, justice; δίκην λαβεῖν, punish; δίκην δοῦναι, be punished.

δίκαιος, -α, -ον and -ος, -ον, just; δικαίως, with justice.

διόλλυμι, -ολῶ, -ώλεσα, destroy, ruin one's life.

Διόσκοροι, οἱ, the two sons of Zeus, Castor and Polydeuces.

δισσός, -ή, -όν, twofold, two.

δμωίς, -ίδος, ἡ, handmaiden.

δοκέω, seem, think; δοκεῖ, it seems good, is resolved; οἱ δοκοῦντες, men of weight.

δόλος, ὁ, craft, strategy.

δόμος, ὁ, house, home.

δόξα, ἡ, expectation, opinion, hope, view.

δορίκτητος, -ον, won by the spear, with gen. dependent on κτῆμα in δορίκτητος, the spear-won spoil of . . .

δόρυ, -ατος or δορός, τό, spear.

δούλη, ἡ, handmaid, bondwoman.

δοῦλος, ὁ, slave; c. gen. a slave to, bound hand and foot by.

δουλόσυνος, -ον, enslaved.

δράω, do, commit.

δύναμαι, -ήσομαι, ἐδυν σάμην, am able.

δύσμαχος, -ον, hard to fight with, invincible.

δυσμενής, -ές, hostile.

δύσνοια, ἡ, illwill, malevolence.

δύστηνος, -ον, unhappy.

δυστυχέω, am ill-fated.

δυστυχής, -ές, ill-fated.

δυσχλαινία, ἡ, mean raiment.

δῶμα, -ατος, τό, house.

Δωρίς, -ίδος, fem. adj. Dorian.

ἐάω, allow, suffer, let be, leave untouched; imper. ἔα, used as exclam. of surprise.

ἐγγύς, adv. near.

ἔγχος, τό, spear.

ἐγώ, ἔγωγε, ἐμοῦ, I.

εἰ, conj. if; εἴπερ, if, as is the case.

εἶεν, particle used in passing from one point to another, so be it, enough.

εἴθε, c. opt. would that.

[εἴκω] ἔοικα, perf. with pres. sign. am like, seem.

εἰλάτινος, ἐλάτινος, -η, -ον, of the pine.

εἰμί, ἔσομαι, ἦν, am; ἔστι, it is possible.

εἶμι (fut.), ᾔειν (imperf.), I will go, come.

εἴρημαι, εἶπον, ἐρῶ, v. φημί.

εἷς, μία, ἕν, one, one and the same.

εἰς, prep. c. acc. into, to, with regard to.

εἰσακούω, hear.

εἶτα, then; often indignantis, and then forsooth.

εἴωθα, am wont; partic. εἰωθώς, familiar.

ἐκ, ἐξ, prep. c. gen. from, out of, by the hand of.

Ἑκάβη, ἡ, Hecuba, wife of Priam.

ἕκαστος, -η, -ον, each, in every case.

ἐκβάλλω, -βαλῶ, ἐξέβαλον, throw out, drop, break down, banish.

ἔκβλητος, -ον, cast up.

ἔκγονος, -ον, sprung from, child.

ἐκεῖθεν, adv. thence, from it; τἀκεῖθεν, things yonder.

ἐκεῖνος, -η, -ο, *dem. pron.* that, he, she, it.

ἐκπέμπω, send out.

ἐκποδών, *adv.* out of the way, away.

ἐκτείνω, -τενῶ, ἐξέτεινα, stretch out.

ἐκτήκω, cause to waste *or* pine away ; ἐκτέτηκα, *intrans.* I pine away.

Ἕκτωρ, -ορος, ὁ, Hector, son of Priam and Hecuba.

ἐκφέρω, ἐξοίσω, ἐξήνεγκα, cast up.

ἐλάσσων, -ον, *compar.* of ἐλαχύς, less.

Ἕλενος, ὁ, Helenus, the soothsayer, son of Priam and Hecuba.

ἐλεύθερος, -α, -ον *and* -ος, -ον, free, knowing not slavery.

Ἑλλάς, -άδος, ἡ, Hellas, the mainland of Greece.

Ἕλλην, -ηνος, ὁ, a Greek.

Ἑλληνικός, -ή, -όν, Greek.

ἐλπίζω, hope.

ἐλπίς, -ίδος, ἡ, hope.

ἐμαυτοῦ, -ῆς, -οῦ, *reflex. pron.* of myself.

ἐμός, -ή, -όν, my, mine.

ἔμπαλιν, *adv.* reversely ; τοὔμπαλιν, the reverse, the reverse is true.

ἐμποδών, *adv.* in the way, opposing, thwarting.

ἐν, *prep. c. dat.* in, among.

ἐναλλάσσω, -αλλάξω, -ήλλαξα, exchange, give instead.

ἐναντίος, -α, -ον, opposite, in the face.

ἐνδίδωμι, give, afford.

ἔνθα, *adv.* where.

ἐνθένδε, *adv.* hence, from here, forthwith.

ἐνθνῄσκω, -θανοῦμαι, -έθανον, die in *or* upon, grow dead and numb.

ἐντίθημι, -θήσω, -έθηκα, put in *or* under, restore, spread in.

ἔνυπνος, -ον, seen in sleep.

ἐξαιτέω, request.

ἐξαλλάσσω, take by way of exchange, take anew.

ἐξέρχομαι, -ελεύσομαι, -ῆλθον, come forth, come.

ἔξεστι, it is lawful, one may.

ἐξευρίσκω, -ευρήσω, -ηῦρον, find.

ἐξιστορέω, inquire from, ask.

ἐξοικίζω, empty, dispeople.

ἔξω, *adv. and prep. c. gen.* outside, outside of.

ἐπαίρω, raise.

ἐπαρκέω, -έσω, help.

ἐπεί, *conj.* when, since.

ἔπειμι, -έσομαι, -ῆν, am set over, preside.

ἔπειτα, *adv.* thereafter.

ἐπερείδω, drive against ; ἐπερείδομαι, am braced up.

ἐπεσπίπτω, -πεσοῦμαι, -έπεσον, burst in upon.

ἐπέχω, ἐφέξω, ἐπέσχον, put off, delay.

ἐπί, *prep. c. acc.* to, in quest of, over ; *c. dat.* in addition to, upon ; *c. gen.* on, towards, in the time of.

ἐπιβαίνω, -βήσομαι, -έβην, set foot upon, mount.

ἐπιζέω, -ζέσω, -έζεσα, bubble up, overwhelm with surge.

ἐπικουρία, ἡ, help, succour.

ἐπιρροθέω, make loud applause.

ἐπισκοπέω, look upon, control.

ἐπιστάτης, -ου, ὁ, presiding over.

ἐπίχειρα, *adv. acc.* on my hands [*alii*, ἐπὶ χεῖρα].

ἔπος, τό, word, tidings.

ἐπωμίς, -ίδος, ἡ, shoulder, shoulder-strap.

ἐράω, love, covet.

ἐργάζομαι, -άσομαι, εἰργασάμην, do.

ἔργον, τό, work, deed.

ἐρημία, ἡ, solitude, being alone.

ἔρημος, -η, -ον *and* -ος, -ον, desolate, forlorn.

ἐρημόω, leave empty, leave.

ἔρχομαι, ἐλεύσομαι, ἦλθον, come.

ἐρωτάω, ask, put question.
ἐσθλός, -ή, -όν, noble, brave.
ἐσοράω, -όψομαι, -εῖδον, look upon, see.
ἑστία, ή, hearth, home.
ἔσω, adv. and prep. c. gen. within.
ἕτερος, -α, -ον, other (of two).
ἔτι, adv. still, further.
ἕτοιμος, -η, -ον and -ος, -ον, ready.
εὖ, adv. well, wisely.
εὐδαίμων, -ον, blessed with good fortune, happy.
εὐδοξία, ή, fair fame, honour.
εὐθύνω, guide straight, rule.
εὐκάρδιος, -ον, stout-hearted.
εὔπαις, -παιδος, ὁ, ή, blessed in his or her children.
εὕρημα, -ατος, τό, invention; λόγων εὑρήματα, words that my lips invented.
Εὐρώπα, Εὐρώπη, ή, Europe.
εὐσεβής, -ές, God-fearing.
εὐσχήμων, -ον, with graceful mien, in seemly wise.
εὔτεκνος, -ον, blessed with goodly offspring.
εὐτρεπής, -ές, turned to meet the stroke, ready.
εὐτυχέω, am blessed with good fortune, prosper.
εὐτυχής, -ές, blessed with good fortune, happy.
ἐφίημι, -ήσω, -ῆκα (paradigm, -ες, -ῶ, -είην, -εῖναι, -είς), lay upon.
ἐφίστημι, ἐπιστήσω, ἐπέστησα, trans. place upon; -έστηκα and [-έσταα] paradigm, -έσταθι, -εστῶ, -εσταίην, -εστάναι, -εστώς, stand at.
ἔχω, ἕξω and σχήσω, ἔσχον, have, hold, threaten, cause, keep.
ἕως, conj. while, until.

ζάω, live.
Ζεύς, Διός, ὁ, Zeus.
ζῆλος, ὁ, rivalry.

ζητέω, seek, desire.
ζυγόν, τό, yoke.

ἤ, or, than; ἤ . . . ἤ, either . . . or.
ἤ, surely, indeed; in questions, can it be that? ἤ γάρ, hast thou really?
ἡγέομαι, ἀγέομαι, lead, guide, consider, believe in, acknowledge.
ἡδέως, adv. sweetly, tenderly.
ἤδη, adv. by now, already, at once.
ἥκιστα, adv. least; no, surely.
ἥκω, ἥξω, am come, come.
ἥλιος, ὁ, the sun. Ἅλιος, the sun-god.
ἦμαρ, -ατος, τό, day.
ἡμεῖς, ἡμῶν, we.
ἡμέρα, ή, day, life.
ἤν = ἐάν, if.
ἡνίκα, when.
ἥσυχος, -ον, still, with quiet voice.
Ἠχώ, -οῦς, ή, Echo.

θάλαμος, ὁ, chamber.
θαλάσσιος, -α, -ον and -ος, -ον, of the sea.
θανάσιμος, -ον, deadly, fatal.
θαρσέω, am confident, am of good courage.
θαῦμα, -ατος, τό, wonder, surprise, wonderment.
θαυμάζω, am surprised, marvel.
θεῖος, -α, -ον, divine, inspired.
θέλω, am willing.
θεόδμητος, -ον, built by or for a god, holy.
θεός, ὁ, god.
θεράπνα, θεράπνη, ή, dwelling, abode.
θῆλυς, θήλεια, θῆλυ, of womankind.
θήρ, θηρός, ὁ, wild beast.
θησαυρός, ὁ, treasure.
θιγγάνω, touch.
θνήσκω, θανοῦμαι, ἔθανον, die.
θνητός, -ή, -όν and -ός, -όν, mortal.
θοός, -ή, -όν, swift.

θόρυβος, ὁ, confused noise, clamour, outcry.

Θρήκη, ἡ, Thrace, i. e. the Thracian Chersonese.

Θρήκιος, -α, -ον, Thracian.

θρηνέω, lament.

θρῆνος, ὁ, lamentation.

Θρῆξ, -κός, ὁ, Thracian.

θυγάτηρ, -τέρος, -τρός, ἡ, daughter.

θῦμα, -ατος, τό, sacrifice.

θυμός, ὁ, spirit, fury.

θυμόομαι, am wroth; τὸ θυμούμενον, angriness, 'thine angry spirit'.

θωύσσω, utter.

Ἰδαῖος, -α, -ον, of Ida, Trojan.

ἴδιος, -α, -ον and -ος, -ον, private, belonging to oneself alone.

ἱερεύς, -έως, ὁ, priest.

ἱερός, -ά, -όν and -ός, -όν, sacred.

Ἰλιάς, -άδος, ἡ, woman of Ilium or Troy.

Ἴλιον, τό, Ilium, the city of Ilos, Troy.

ἵνα, conj. in order that; adv. where.

ἱππότας, ἱππότης, -οῦ, ὁ, horseman, knight.

ἴσος, -η, -ον, equal, the same, fair.

ἵστημι, στήσω, ἔστησα, place; ἔστην, ἔστηκα, stand, stand idle.

ἴσχω, hold, stop.

ἴχνος, -ους, τό, track, footstep; κατ᾽ ἴχνος, on the trail.

καθαιμάσσω, defile with blood.

καθαιρέω, -αιρήσω, -εῖλον, bring low, vanquish.

καθίημι, -ήσω, -ῆκα (partic. καθείς), put down, rest.

καί, and, even, also; καὶ γάρ, for in fact; καὶ μήν, and look you.

καινός, -ή, -όν, fresh, new-fashioned.

κακός, -ή, -όν, evil; κακίων, comp. worse, baser; κακόν, an evil, woe, reproach.

καλέω, -έσω, ἐκάλεσα, call, name.

καλός, -ή, -όν, beauteous, fair, noble, good, honourable; καλῶς, κάλλιον, κάλλιστα, adv. well, happily, nobly; ἐστὶν καλῶς, apparently = ἔχει καλῶς, is well.

κάμνω, suffer, fail, err, labour, am distressed.

καπνός, ὁ, smoke.

κάρα, τό, head, face.

καρδία, ἡ, heart.

καρτερέω, am patient, persist in.

Κασάνδρα, ἡ, daughter of Priam and Hecuba, gifted by Apollo with prophetic powers.

κάσις, ὁ, ἡ, brother, sister.

κατά, prep. c. gen. down upon, down from, against; c. acc. according to, over; κατ᾽ ἦμαρ, from day to day.

καταθνήσκω, -θανοῦμαι, -έθανον, die, am slain.

κατακτείνω, -κτενῶ, -έκτεινα, str. aor. κατέκταν, slay.

κατάρατος, -ον, accursed, infamous.

κατασκάπτω, str. aor. pass. -εσκάφην, raze to the ground.

κατάσκοπος, ὁ, spy.

καταστάζω, bedew, drop upon.

κατεῖπον, I denounced, told.

κατερείπω, cast down; pass. am falling in ruin.

κατέχω, possess, dwell in.

κεῖμαι, lie; used as pass. of τίθημι, am placed, stand; passed, laid down (of a law).

κεῖνος, -η, -ο, demonstr. that yonder, he, she, it.

κελεύω, advise, bid.

κέλλω, κέλσω, ἔκελσα, put in to shore, find harbourage.

κενός, -ή, -όν, empty, free from.

κερκίς, -ίδος, ἡ, the comb used in weaving, the loom.

κευθμών, -ῶνος, ὁ, hiding place, dark recess.

κεύθω, κεύσω, ἔκευσα, κέκευθα, conceal.

κίνδυνος, ὁ, danger, risk.

Κισσεύς, ὁ, a Thracian prince, father of Hecuba.

κλέος, τό, repute, honour.

κλύδων, -ωνος, ὁ, billow.

κλύω, hear.

κοινός, -ή, -όν and -ός, -όν, common, hospitable.

κομίζω, bring, lead, waft.

κομιστήρ, -ῆρος, ὁ, one who leads, conductor, escort.

κόμπος, ὁ, boast, boastful words.

κόνις, -ιος and -εως, ἡ, dust.

κορή, ἡ, maiden, daughter, pupil of the eye.

κορμός, ὁ, trunk, log.

κόσμος, ὁ, ornament.

κραίνω, κρανῶ, ἔκρανα, wk. aor. pass. ἐκράνθην, resolve upon, ratify.

κρατέω, rule, prevail, am superior in power.

κράτος, -ους, τό, superior power, authority, power to subdue.

κραυγή, ἡ, outcry.

κρίνω, κρινῶ, ἔκρινα, judge, decide, interpret.

κρουνός, ὁ, spring, stream.

κρύπτω, wk. aor. pass. ἐκρύφθην, hide, veil, bury.

κρύφιος, -α, -ον and -ος, -ον, hidden, by stealth.

κτάομαι, κτήσομαι, ἐκτησάμην, κέκτημαι, wk. aor. pass. ἐκτήθην, get, possess, buy.

κτείνω, slay.

κτύπος, ὁ, noise.

κῦμα, -ατος, τό, wave.

κυρέω, light upon, find.

λαγών, -όνος, ἡ, flank, side.

λάθρᾳ, adv. in secret, by stealth.

λαῖφος, -ους, τό, sail.

λαιψηρός, -ά, -όν, nimble.

Λάκαινα, ἡ, fem. of Λάκων, a Laconian or Spartan woman.

λαμβάνω, λήψομαι, ἔλαβον, take, seize.

λαμπρός, -ά, -όν, bright.

λαός, ὁ, people, folk.

λάσκω, ἔλακον, λέλακα, utter aloud, make one's voice heard.

λέγω, λέξω, ἔλεξα, say, speak.

λεηλατέω, drive off the spoil, harry.

λείπω, λείψω, ἔλιπον, leave.

λέκτρον, τό, bed; ἐπὶ λέκτρα, to wed.

λευρός, -ά, -όν, smooth.

λέχος, -ους, τό, bed.

Λῆμνος, ἡ, Lemnos, an island in the Aegean.

λίμνη, ἡ, lake, sea.

λιπαίνω, enrich.

λίσσομαι, entreat, make supplication.

λόγος, ὁ, word, speech.

λοιδορέω, abuse, say aught that may offend.

λύπη, ἡ, pain, sorrow.

λυπρός, -ά, -όν, painful, sorrowful, vexatious.

λύω, loosen; λύεται μέλη, limbs fail.

μάθημα, -ατος, τό, learning.

μακρός, -ά, -όν, long, long drawn out.

μάλα, adv. very; μάλ' αὖθις, yet again; comp. μᾶλλον, more, rather; superl. μάλιστα, most, assuredly.

μανθάνω, μαθήσομαι, ἔμαθον, learn, perceive, know.

μαργάω, rage, am frenzied.

μάρπτω, μάρψω, ἔμαρψα, seize.

μαστός, ὁ, breast.

ματεύω, search, seek after knowledge.

μάτην, adv. in vain, to no purpose.

μάτηρ, v. μήτηρ.

μαχέομαι, fight.

μέγας, μεγάλη, μέγα, great, grievous ; *superl.* μέγιστος, greatest; μέγα, very.

μεθίημι, -ήσω, -ῆκα (*paradigm*, -ες, -ῶ, -είην, -εῖναι, -είς), cast, unhand, let be, let, leave.

μείζων, -ον, *compar. of* μέγας, greater, worse ; μειζόνως, *adv.* worse.

μελανόπτερος, -ον, black-winged.

μέλεος, -α, -ον *and* -ος, -ον, unhappy.

μέλλω, hesitate, delay.

μέλος, τό, (*always in plur.*), a limb. μέλος, τό, song, strain, dirge.

μέμνημαι, remember.

μέμφομαι, find fault with, blame, think not highly of.

μέν, *particle, commonly used to contrast the word before it with another followed by* δέ.

μέντοι, however.

μέριμνα, ή, care, anxiety ; δισσὴ μέριμνα, the two that share my thoughts.

μέρος, -ους, τό, heritage, lot ; ἐν μέρει, in turn.

μέσος, -η, -ον, middle, middle of, mid ; μέσως, *adv.* in moderate wise.

μετά, *prep. c. acc.* after ; *c. gen.* with ; *c. dat.* with, among.

μεταξύ, *adv.* between, in the interval ; *prep. c. gen.* between.

μετάρσιος, -ον *and* -α, -ον, raised aloft, up.

μέτειμι, am among ; *impers.* μέτεστί μοι, I have a share in, I have part or lot in.

μή, *adv. of negation with imperat., in condit. and final clauses, with most infinitives,* not, lest.

μηδέ, and not, nor, not even.

μηδείς, μηδεμία, μηδέν, not even one, no one, nothing.

μήν, *particle used to strengthen*

protestations, &c. ; καὶ μήν, and lo ! and look you !

μήτε, neither, nor.

μήτηρ, μητρός, ή, mother.

μιαιφόνος, -ον, blood-stained, murderous.

μισθός, ό, pay, reward, fee.

μόνος, -η, -ον, alone, only ; μόνον, *adv.* only.

μόρος, ό, doom, destiny, fate.

μοχθέω, labour.

μῦθος, ό, word, message.

μυχός, ό, inmost corner, inner chamber.

ναυστολέω, go on shipboard, sail.

νεανίας, -ου, ό, youth, young man.

νεᾶνις, -ιδος, ή, girl, maiden.

νεκρός, ό, dead body, corse ; νεκροί, the dead.

νέμω, deal out ; πλέον νέμειν, pay too much heed.

νέος, -α, -ον *and* -ος, -ον, new, young, fresh.

νεοσφαγής, -ές, newly slain.

νέρθεν, *adv. and prep. c. gen.* below, beneath.

νιν, *enclitic acc. of 3rd pers., poetic. for* αὐτόν, αὐτήν, αὐτό.

νόμος, ό, custom, law.

νύμφη, ή, bride.

νῦν, *adv.* now ; νῦν δέ, but as it is, as things are.

νῶτον, τό, back.

ξενία, ή, hospitality.

ξενοκτονέω, slay a guest.

ξένος, ξεῖνος, ό, guest, friend.

ξίφος, -ους, τό, sword.

ξυγκλείω, ξυγκλήω, -ήσω, wrap, muffle.

ξύνειμι, -έσομαι, -ῆν, am with, on the side of.

ξύνοδος, ή, assembly.

ξυνοικίζω, join in peopling.

ὁ, ή, τό, *def. art.* the ; *with* μέν *and* δέ *it may be demonstrative* ; ὁ μὲν ... ὁ δέ, one ... another.

ὀγκόω, raise up; ὀγκοῦμαι, am puffed up with pride.

ὅδε, ἥδε, τόδε, demonstr. pron., this, the following; τάνδε, sc. ὁδόν, this way, this direction.

ὄδυρμα, -ατος, τό, lamentation.

Ὀδυσσεύς, -έως, ὁ, Odysseus (Ulysses), king of Ithaca.

οἴ, exclamation of pain, οἲ 'γώ, woe is me!

οἶδα, εἴσομαι, ᾔδη or ᾔδειν, know.

οἶδμα, -ατος, τό, swollen waves.

οἰκίζω, people; perf. pass. ᾤκισται, hath made his abode.

οἶκος, ὁ, house, family.

οἰκτίζω, -ίσω, ᾤκτισα, have pity.

οἰκτίρω, οἰκτείρω, have pity, show compassion.

οἶκτος, ὁ, pity.

οἴμοι, exclamation of pain or grief, ah me!

οἰμωγή, ἡ, wailing, lamentation.

οἷος, οἵα, οἷον, relative, of what sort, how grievous; οἷός περ, just what; οἷός τε εἰμί, I am such a person as to = I am able to.

οἴχομαι, am gone, lost, undone.

ὄλβιος, -α, -ον and -ος, -ον, happy, blest.

ὄλλυμι, ὀλέσω, ὀλῶ, ὤλεσα, ruin, destroy, slay; midd. with perf. ὄλωλα, perish.

ὄμμα, -ατος, τό, eye.

ὀμφαλός, ὁ, navel.

ὅμως, however, still, yet.

ὄνειρον, τό, ὄνειρος, ὁ, dream.

ὀνειρόφρων, -ονος, ὁ, ἡ, versed in the lore of dreams.

ὄνησις, -εως, ἡ, benefit, advantage.

ὀνίνημι, ὀνίναμαι, aor. ὠνάμην, have profit from, enjoy.

ὄνομα, -ατος, τό, name.

ὀπάων, -ονος, ὁ, comrade, attendant.

ὅπλον, τό, weapon, arm.

ὅπως, adv. how; conj. in order that.

ὁράω, ὄψομαι, εἶδον, see; midd.

εἰδόμην in same sense, imperat. ἰδοῦ, behold, mark; ἰδού, lo! pass aor. ὤφθην, was seen.

ὄρειος, -α, -ον and -ος, -ον, haunting the hills.

ὀρέστερος, -α, -ον, of the hills.

ὀρθός, -ή, -όν, straight, upright, unmoved, high-raised.

ὁρίζω, set limits to, define, mark out.

ὅρισμα, -ατος, τό, boundary, landmark.

ὁρμάω, set in motion; ὁρμάομαι, am hurled, dealt.

ὅρμος, ὁ, roadstead, haven.

ὅρος, ὁ, boundary; ὅροι, territory.

ὅς, ἥ, ὅ, relative, who, which; ὅ = δι' ὅ, wherefore.

ὅσιος, -α, -ον and -ος, -ον, holy, pious, righteous.

ὅσος, -η, -ον, relative, how many, how much, how great; ὅσον περ, even as long as.

ὅσπερ, ἥπερ, ὅπερ, the very man who, the very thing that.

ὅστε = ὅς.

ὅστις, ἥτις, ὅ τι, gen. οὕτινος or ὅτου, dat. ᾧτινι or ὅτῳ, relative, who, whoever.

ὅταν, when, whenever.

ὅτε, when.

οὐ, οὐκ, οὐχ, οὐχί, not, no.

οὗ, relat. adv. where.

οὐδέ, neither, nor, not even.

οὐδείς, οὐδεμία, οὐδέν, not even one, no one, nothing.

οὐκέτι, no longer.

οὔκουν, not then; οὐκοῦν, then.

οὖν, adv. of inference, then.

οὕνεκα, rel. conj. for which purpose, prep. c. gen. on account of.

οὔποτε, never.

οὔτε ... οὔτε, neither ... nor.

οὔτις, οὔτι, no one, nothing; οὔτι, in no wise.

οὗτος, αὕτη, τοῦτο, demonstr. pron. this; voc. οὗτος, you, there! ταύταν, sc. ὁδόν, this way.

οὔτω, οὔτως, *adv.* thus, so.
ὄχλος, ὁ, crowd, the masses.
ὄψ, ὀπός, ἡ, voice.
ὄψις, -εως, ἡ, vision.

πᾷ, *sc.* ὁδῷ, in which direction?
παῖς, παιδός, ὁ, ἡ, son, daughter, child.
παίω, παίσω, ἔπαισα, strike.
πάλιν, *adv.* again, backwards; πάλιν τε καὶ πρόσω, to and fro.
πάλλευκος, -ον, all-white, hoary.
παρά, *prep. c. gen.* from ; *c. dat.* by the side of, in the house of, with ; *c. acc.* to the side of, to, along, contrary to; πάρα = πάρεστι.
παραβαίνω, -βήσομαι, -έβην, go by, escape.
παρακαλέω, call, summon.
παράφορος, -ον, staggering.
πάρειμι, am present, ready; τὸ παρόν, what I have.
παρέχω, -έξω *and* παρασχήσω, -έσχον, cause.
παρηγορέω, counsel, turn from their purpose.
παρθένος, ἡ, maiden.
παρίστημι, *trans.* set near ; *pass. with* παρέστην, παρέστηκα, *intrans.* stand near, am present, have come.
πάρος, *adv. and prep. c. gen.* before, in front of.
παρουσία, ἡ, presence.
πᾶς, πᾶσα, πᾶν, all, the whole, every.
πάσχω, πείσομαι, ἔπαθον, πέπονθα, experience, suffer.
πατήρ, πατρός, ὁ, father.
πάτριος, -α, -ον *and* -ος, -ον, of one's father, a father's.
πατρῷος, -α, -ον *and* -ος, -ον, of *or* from one's father.
πεδίον, τό, plain.
πείθω, persuade.
Πειθώ, -οῦς, ἡ, Persuasion (*personified*).

πελάγιος, -α, -ον *and* -ος, -ον, of the sea, on the open sea.
πελάζω, approach ; *aor. pass.* ἐπλάθην, *in same meaning.*
πέλας, *adv.* (*with gen. or dat.*) near.
πέμπω, πέμψω, ἔπεμψα, send ; *midd.* send for.
πένομαι, am poor and needy.
πέπλος, ὁ, garb, raiment.
πέρα, *adv.* beyond, transcending.
περί, *prep. c. gen.* about, concerning ; *c. dat.* round about ; *c. acc.* about.
πέριξ, *adv. and prep.* all round, round about.
περιπίπτω, -πεσοῦμαι, -έπεσον, fall in with, am involved in.
περιπτύσσω, wrap.
περισσός, -ή, -όν, excessive ; περισσά, beyond all others, signally.
πέσημα, -ατος, τό, fall ; πέσημα δορός, laid low by the spear.
πέτρα, ἡ, rock, cliff.
πεύκινος, -η, -ον, of pine.
πῆμα, -ατος, τό, woe, misery.
πημονά, πημονή, ἡ, suffering.
πίπτω (πίτνω), πεσοῦμαι, ἔπεσον, fall.
πιστός, -ή, -όν, faithful, sure, assured.
πλάξ, πλακός, ἡ, table-land, plain.
πλευρά, -ᾶς, ἡ, rib, side.
πλέων, -ον, *comp. of* πολύς, more.
πλῆθος, -ους, τό, multitude, masses, commons, numbers.
πλήν, *prep. c. gen. and adv.* except, save.
πλήρης, -ες, full.
πληρόω, fill, pile high.
πλησίον, *adv.* near, side by side ; ὁ πλησίον, one's neighbour.
πλούσιος, -α, -ον, wealthy.
πνεῦμα, -ατος, τό, breath.
πόθεν, whence ? ποθέν, from somewhere or other.
ποῖ, whither ?

ποιέω, do, make; ποιοῦμαι, render, make.

ποῖος, ποία, ποῖον, what kind of? what? ποίαν, *sc.* ὁδόν, what direction?

πολέμιος, -α, -ον *and* -ος, -ον, hostile; πολέμιος, ὁ, an enemy.

πόλις, -εως *and* -εος, ἡ, city.

πολίτης, -ου, ὁ, citizen.

πολλάκις, *adv.* often.

Πολύδωρος, ὁ, Polydorus, youngest son of Priam.

Πολυμήστωρ, -ορος, ὁ, Polymestor, king of the Thracians.

Πολυξένη, ἡ, Polyxena, daughter of Hecuba.

πολύπονος, -ον, grievously afflicted.

πολύς, πολλή, πολύ, much, many, long; οἱ πολλοί, most; *comp.* πλείων *or* πλέων, *superl.* πλεῖστος.

πολύχρυσος, -ον, rich in gold.

πομπός, ὁ, escort.

πόνος, ὁ, toil, task, suffering, woe.

ποντιάς, -άδος, *fem. adj.* of the ocean.

πόντιος, -α, -ον *and* -ος, -ον, of the sea.

ποντοπόρος, -ον, faring o'er the sea.

πόντος, ὁ, the open sea.

πορεύω, cause to go, carry.

ποτε, *enclitic particle*, at some time or other, at any time, ever.

πότερος, -α, -ον, which of the two; πότερα *or* πότερον ... ἤ, whether ... or, is this the case, or that?

πότμος, ὁ, lot, destiny, doom.

ποῦ, where? που, somewhere, anywhere, I suppose.

πούς, ποδός, ὁ, foot.

πρᾶγμα, -ατος, τό, thing, matter, question, deed.

πράσσω, πράξω, ἔπραξα, do, accomplish; εὖ πράσσειν, fare well, be in prosperity.

Πριαμίδης, ὁ, son of Priam.

Πρίαμος, ὁ, Priam, son of Laomedon, king of Troy.

πρίν, *conj.* before, until; *adv.* formerly.

προθυμέομαι, am eager, desire.

πρόθυμος, -ον, zealous, patriotic.

προκόπτω, cut a way in front, make way ahead.

προλείπω, faint.

προμηθία, ἡ, forethought, deliberate purpose.

πρόνοια, ἡ, care.

πρός, *prep. c. gen.* from, at the hand of; πρὸς θεῶν, in heaven's name; *c. dat.* in addition to; *c. acc.* to, at, against, with reference to.

προσβλέπω, look at, look another in the face.

προσεῖπον, address.

πρόσθεν, *adv.* formerly, in advance, to the front.

προστίθημι, -θήσω, -έθηκα (*partic.* -θείς), put to, impose, yield, dedicate.

προσφιλής, -ές, dear.

πρόσφορος, -ον, suitable, to suit one's purpose.

πρόσω, *adv.* forward; πάλιν τε καὶ πρόσω, to and fro.

πρότονοι, οἱ, forestays.

πρῶτος, -η, -ον, first, most prominent, chiefest; πρῶτον, τὸ πρῶτον, πρῶτα, *used adverbially*, first, in the first place.

πτόλις, *v.* πόλις.

πτόρθος, ὁ, branch, sapling.

πτώσσω, cower.

πύλη, ἡ, gate, portal.

πυρά, ἡ, funeral pyre.

πύργος, ὁ, tower.

πω, yet.

πῶς, how? πως, in a way.

ῥᾴδιος, -α, -ον *and* -ος, -ον, easy, light.

ῥέω, flow, rush, hurl oneself.
ῥήγνυμι, ῥήξω, ἔρρηξα, rend.

σαίρω, sweep.
σάλος, ὁ, tossing, rolling swell of the sea.
σαυτοῦ, σαυτῆς, σαυτοῦ, *reflex. pron. 2nd pers.* of thyself.
σαφής, -ές, clear, clearly seen.
σέβω, worship.
σέθεν, *v.* σύ.
σημαίνω, σημανῶ, ἐσήμηνα, make known, show.
σθένω, am strong, carry weight.
σιγάω, am silent, say no more.
σιδάρεος (σιδήρεος), -οῦς, -ᾶ, -οῦν, of iron.
σίδηρος, ὁ, iron, 'the steel'.
σιτοποιός, ὁ, ἡ, *adj.* bread-making, of preparing corn.
σκηνή, ἡ, tent ; *plur.* camp.
σκότος, ὁ, gloom; the nether world.
σμικρός, -ά, -όν, small.
σός, σή, σόν, thy.
σοφός, -ή, -όν, wise.
σπανίζω, have any lack of.
σπάνις, -εως, ἡ, scarcity, lack.
σπείρω, sow, farm.
σπουδάζω, am eager, earnestly endeavour.
σπουδή, ἡ, eagerness, speed.
σταλαγμός, ὁ, dropping, drop.
στέγη, ἡ, roof, dwelling.
στείχω, go, move.
στέλλω, make ready ; *midd.* prepare to go, start.
στεναγμός, ὁ, groaning, lamentation.
στέργω, am content.
στερέω, deprive ; *str. aor. pass. partic.* στερείς, robbed of.
στέρνον, τό, breast.
στερρός, -ά, -όν and -ός, -όν, hard, unfeeling.
στόλος, ὁ, expedition, armada.
στράτευμα, -ατος, τό, army.
στρατός, ὁ, army.
σύ, σοῦ and σέθεν, *pron. 2nd sing.* thou.

σύγγονος, -ον, akin ; σύγγονος, *as noun*, brother, sister.
συγκλῄω, close, wrap, huddle.
συμβούλομαι, join in one's wish, give assent.
σύμμαχος, -ον, fighting with, in alliance with.
συμπίτνω, fall in with, come opportunely.
συμφορά, ἡ, misfortune.
σύν, *prep. c. dat.* with.
συνδράω, take active part with.
σύνοιδα, know with another, am privy to.
σφαγή, ἡ, slaughter, slaying, murderous stroke.
σφάγιον, τό, victim, offering.
σφάζω, σφάξω, ἔσφαξα, *strong aor. pass.* ἐσφάγην, slay.
σχεδία, ἡ, raft, ship.
σχές, *v.* ἔχω.
σχῆμα, -ατος, τό, outline, familiar shape.
σχολάζω, delay.
σῴζω, save.
σῶμα, -ατος, τό, body.

ταλαίπωρος, -ον, distressed, poor wretch.
τάλας, τάλαινα, τάλαν, miserable, unhappy.
Ταλθύβιος, ὁ, herald of Agamemnon.
ταπεινός, -ή, -όν, humble.
ταραγμός, ὁ, confusion.
ταρβέω, am alarmed, tremble with fear.
τάσσω, appoint.
τάφος, ὁ, tomb.
τάχα, *adv.* θᾶσσον, τάχιστα, quickly ; ὡς τάχιστα, as soon as ; τάχα, *and more commonly* τάχ' ἄν, perhaps.
τε, *enclitic particle*, and ; τε . . . καί, both . . . and.
τεῖχος, -ους, τό, wall.
τέκνον, τό, child.

τέκος, -ους, τό, child.

τέλος, -ους, τό, end; ἐς τέλος, unto perfection, thoroughly.

τέμνω, τεμῶ, ἔτεμον, aor. midd. ἐταμόμην, cut, fell.

τετράπους, -πουν, four-footed, a four-footed beast.

τίκτω, τέξω, ἔτεκον, bear; ἡ τεκοῦσα, the mother.

τίθημι, θήσω, ἔθηκα, place, make; aor. midd. ἐθέμην; χάριν θέσθαι, lay up gratitude, put under obligation; ἐν αἰσχρῷ θέσθαι, account disgraceful.

τιμάω, honour.

τιμή, ἡ, honour.

τίμιος, -α, -ον and -ος, -ον, honoured.

τιμωρέω, help; τιμωρέομαι, avenge.

τιμωρός, -όν, helping, avenging, an avenger.

τις, τι, indef. pron. any one, anything, some one, a ; τι, somewhat.

τίς, τί, interrog. pron. who? what? τί, why?

[τλάω], ἔτλην, dared, ventured; imperat. τλῆθι, endure, be content to suffer.

τλήμων, τλάμων, -ον, enduring, wretched, afflicted.

τοι, enclitic particle, be sure, thou must know.

τοιόσδε, τοιάδε, τοιόνδε, such, the following.

τοιοῦτος, τοιαύτη, τοιοῦτο and τοιοῦτον, such, so great.

τόλμα, ἡ, daring, act of daring.

τολμάω, dare, venture, have the hardihood, bring oneself to.

τότε, adv. at that time, then.

τράπεζα, ἡ, table.

τρέφω, θρέψω, ἔθρεψα, wk. aor. pass. ἐθρέφθην, rear, nurture, nurse, prolong life.

τρίβω, harass, ravage.

τριταῖος, -α, -ον, on the third day, third.

Τροία, ἡ, Troy, city of Phrygia.

τρόπος, ὁ, way, fashion, line of action.

τροφή, ἡ, nourishment, nurture.

Τρωάς, fem. adj. Trojan, Trojan dame.

Τρῶες, -ων, οἱ, Trojans.

Τρωικός, -ή, -όν, Trojan.

τυγχάνω, τεύξομαι, ἔτυχον, fall in with, find, meet with, happen, win one's point; with partic. happen to . . .

τύμβος, ὁ, tomb.

τύραννος, ὁ, ἡ, lord, despot, monarch, sovereign.

τυφλός, -ή, -όν, blind, wandering (as in darkness).

τυφλόω, blind.

τύφω, raise a smoke; τύφομαι, smoke, smoulder.

τύχη, ἡ, fortune, fate, ill-luck, chance; Τύχη, Misfortune (personified).

τῷ = τίνι.

ὕδωρ, -ατος, τό, water, stream.

ὕλη, ὕλα, wood, timber, forest.

ὑμεῖς, -ῶν, ye.

ὑπάρχω, am to begin with, am in store or reserve.

ὑπεκπέμπω, -πέμψω, ὑπεξέπεμψα, send out by stealth.

ὑπεξάγω, withdraw furtively, withdraw.

ὑπέρ, prep. c. gen. over, over the head of, in defence of ; c. acc. beyond, contrary to.

ὑπερθρώσκω, leap or rise above.

ὑπό, prep. c. gen. from under, by, by reason of; c. dat. under ; c. acc. under, at.

ὕποπτος, -ον, suspecting, suspicious of.

ὕστατος, -η, -ον, last.

φαίνομαι, φανοῦμαι, ἐφάνην, appear, am shown.

φάος, -ους, φῶς, φωτός, τό, light, light of day.

φάρμακον, τό, drug, poison.

φάσγανον, τό, sword.

φάσμα, -ατος, τό, appearance, vision.

φέγγος, -ους, τό, light, day, light of the eyes, sight.

φείδομαι, spare.

φέρω, οἴσω, ἤνεγκα *and* ἤνεγκον, bear, endure, bring tidings, carry off (as plunder); φέρομαι, get for oneself, win.

φεῦ, *exclamation*, alas!

φεύγω, φεύξομαι, φευξοῦμαι, ἔφυγον, fly, escape.

φήμη, φάμα, ἡ, talk, report.

φημί, φήσω *or* ἐρῶ, εἶπον, εἴρηκα; *pass.*εἴρημαι,ἐρρήθην,say,speak.

Φθιάς, -άδος, *fem. adj.* of Phthia, Phthian.

φθονέω, envy, grudge.

φθόνος, ὁ, envy, a thing invidious, evoking the anger of heaven.

φίλιππος, -ον, horse-loving.

φίλος, -η, -ον, dear, beloved; *as noun*, a friend; *superl.* φίλτατος.

φιλοψυχέω, cherish one's life, play the coward.

φλόξ, φλογός, ἡ, flame, fire.

φόβος, ὁ, alarm.

φοίνιος, -α, -ον, blood-stained, murderous.

φονεύς, φονέως, ὁ, murderer.

φόνος, ὁ, bloodshed, murder, blood.

φορέω, toss.

φράζω, φράσω, ἔφρασα, say, tell, explain.

φρήν, φρενός, ἡ, mind, heart, spirit, disposition.

φρίσσω, shudder.

φρονέω, think, feel, cherish (thoughts).

φρόνημα, -ατος, τό, high thoughts, pride.

φροντίς, -ίδος, ἡ, thought, imagination.

φρουρέω, keep safe, guard.

Φρύγες, -ῶν, οἱ, Phrygians.

φυλακή, ἡ, safe-keeping.

φύλλον, τό, leaf, leafy spray.

φύρω, sully, defile, confuse.

φύω, φύσω, ἔφυσα (*trans.*), produce; πέφυκα, ἔφυν (*intrans.*), was born.

φωνή, ἡ, voice.

φώς, φωτός, ὁ, man.

χαίρω, rejoice, am in sympathy with; *imperat.* hail, farewell.

χάρις, -ιτος, ἡ, favour; χάριν τινός, for a man's sake, ἐμὴν χάριν, for my sake.

χείρ, χειρός *and* χερός, ἡ, hand.

Χερσονήσιος, -α, -ον, of the Chersonese, *i.e.* the Thracian Chersonese, on the Hellespont.

χθόνιος, -α, -ον *and* -ος, -ον, beneath the earth, of the Under World.

χθών, χθονός, ἡ, land, country.

χιονώδης, -ες, snowy.

χραίνω, defile, dishonour.

χράομαι, use, enjoy, treat as ...

χρεία, ἡ, need.

χρέος, -ους, τό, debt, behoof; σὸν χρέος, for thy sake.

χρή, χρήσει, ἐχρῆν *or* χρῆν, χρεών (*sc.* ἐστί), it behoves, one must, it is fated.

χρήζω, wish, am eager.

χρῆμα, -ατος, τό, thing, matter; τί χρῆμα, why? χρήματα, wealth.

χρηστός, -ή, -όν, good, successful, virtuous; τὰ χρηστά, prosperity.

χρόνος, ὁ, time.

χρύσεος, -έα, -εον, -οῦς, -ῆ, -οῦν, golden.

χρυσός, ὁ, gold.

χρυσοφαής, -ές, with golden light.

χρώς, χρωτός *and* χροός, ὁ, skin, flesh.

χῶμα, -ατος, τό, mound.

χωρέω, go, depart, flow, come.

χωρίς, *adv.* apart.

ψάμαθος, ἡ, sand of the shore.

ψαύω, ψαύσω, ἔψαυσα, touch, move to pity.
ψευδής, -ές, false, unfounded.
ψῆφος, ἡ, pebble, vote, decree.
ψόγος, ὁ, blame.
ψυχή, ἡ, life, soul, spirit, prophetic spirit.

ὤ, *exclamation of surprise, pain, joy.*
ὦ, *with voc., mark of address.*
ὧδε, *adv.* thus.

ὤμοι, *exclamation,* ah me !
ὠμός, -ή, -όν, cruel, harsh.
ὠνέομαι, purchase.
ὠνητός, -ή, -όν *and* -ός, -όν, bought.
ὡς, *conj.* in order that ; *adv.* as, how, when ; ὡς τάχιστα, as soon as ; ὡς = πρός, to (*of persons*).
ὥς, would that.
ὥστε, *conj.* so as to, so that ; *adv.* as.

PRINTED IN ENGLAND
AT THE OXFORD UNIVERSITY PRESS